CHINA'S SPACE CAPABILITIES

ANAND V.

Introduction by
Air Commodore **Jasjit Singh** AVSM, VrC, VM (Retd)

KNOWLEDGE WORLD

KW Publishers Pvt Ltd
New Delhi

in association with

Centre for Air Power Studies
New Delhi

2011 FPBA BEST PUBLISHERS AWARD (ENGLISH)

The Centre for Air Power Studies is an independent, non-profit, academic research institution established in 2002 under a registered Trust to undertake and promote policy-related research, study and discussion on the trends and developments in defence and military issues, especially air power and the aerospace arena, for civil and military purposes. Its publications seek to expand and deepen the understanding of defence, military power, air power and aerospace issues without necessarily reflecting the views of any institution or individuals except those of the authors.

Jasjit Singh
Director General
Centre for Air Power Studies
P-284, Arjan Path
Subroto Park
New Delhi 110010

Tele: (91-11) 25699131
E-mail: diroffice@aerospaceindia.org

Published in India by
Kalpana Shukla
KW Publishers Pvt Ltd
4676/21, First Floor, Ansari Road, Daryaganj, New Delhi 110002
T: +91 11 23263498/43528107 E: knowledgeworld@vsnl.net • www.kwpub.com

ISBN 978-93-81904-22-0

Printed and bound in India

CONTENTS

Introduction

I feel privileged to introduce the reader to this series of **New Delhi Papers** which contain focused research on one or two issues concerning India's national security and interests. It is also a matter of satisfaction that these objective studies have been carried out mostly by young academic and military scholars (normally below 30 years age) affiliated to this Centre on a 9-month "Non-Resident Fellowship" programme. The details of this programme are to be found at the end of this paper.

National security is a multidisciplinary subject ranging from core values, theory, security interests, challenges, options for management and other aspects covering almost all areas of national enterprise like defence, internal security, economic and technological security etc. all linked in a holistic manner. But unfortunately this is absent in our education system at the hundreds of universities and other teaching establishments. Without adequate education and understanding of national security India's multi-cultural diversity within the liberal democratic freedoms, therefore, tends to only progressively strengthen regionalism and parochialism with far reaching consequences. Hence this modest attempt to fill a serious vacuum in our education system which for three centuries has remained mired in Lord Macaulay's educational model leading to narrowly conceived approach to national imperatives which, by definition, require a broader *national* approach.

I am confident you will enjoy reading this paper and you are welcome to raise comments and critique so that we can improve future efforts. The views expressed in the study are those of the author and do not necessarily reflect those of the Centre or any other institution.

Jasjit Singh
Director General
Centre for Air Power Studies

New Delhi

1. Probing China's Capabilities in Space

Over the years, space programme in China has evolved by achieving significant milestones since its inception in mid-1950s. At the core of China's space programme is its strong satellite programme for which telecommunication, broadcasting, and geo-informatics-related applications became possible; these gave China the required capability to carry out socio-economic, industrial as well as technological developments. Since the launch of the first satellite in 1970, a number of satellites were developed with different specifications and roles. With its base built on the satellite programme, China has gone further ahead and has expanded into other domains like human spaceflight, space exploration, commercial space services and also, space militarization. China became the 3rd nation to send a human to space and also conduct an Anti-Satellite (ASAT) test; it is the 4th nation to launch a lunar probe. These phenomenal developments in space have been used by China not only for enhancing its domestic developments, but also the comprehensive national power. As a result, it will have ramifications in global geopolitics, and especially so for a neighbouring country like India.

In this context, a modest attempt has been made to understand, in greater detail, the space capabilities of China, and also at its implications, with a focus on India. Initially, the origin of China's space programme and its evolution over the decades until the end of 2011 has been explored in brief. The infrastructure facilities of the space programme, which is the key to managing the overall space activities as well as launching spacecrafts and controlling its operations in orbit, has been assessed subsequently. Further, the capabilities China possesses with respect to its various space missions has been evaluated comprehensively. The contemporary issue of weaponisation of space and China's role in it has also been probed to better understand how 'peaceful' China would tend to behave in space with its existing capabilities. The conclusion focusses on ascertaining what the growing capabilities in China's space sector could mean to its counterpart in India, and how India should respond. This has been carried out by conducting a comparative assessment, and thereby, articulating the way forward for India's space programme with respect to that of China.

2. The Emergence of China as a Space-Faring Nation

Not only the Chinese, the origins of the whole of humanity's spacefaring efforts can be traced back to ancient China because it was here that the rocket, the indispensible vehicle for space launches, was conceived. Rockets or 'flying arrows' in Chinese were invented by Feng Jishen in 970 AD, and were powered with gunpowder, yet another Chinese invention. The first Chinese attempt to reach the heaven was made by a 16th century inventor Wan Hu using a rocket propelled chair, which ended in a fatal accident.[1] Thus, the Chinese ambitions of venturing into the domain of outer space are very much rooted in its civilization.

These ambitions re-emerged centuries later in the People's Republic of China (PRC) established by the Communist Party of China (CPC) in 1949 under the chairmanship of Mao Zedong. China's space programme basically emerged out of its ballistic missile programme.[2] Since the establishment of the PRC, Washington developed animosity towards Beijing because they found themselves on opposing sides of various geopolitical developments like the formation of Cold War blocs, the Taiwan issue, and the Korean and Vietnam wars. The US further intimidated the Chinese with 'nuclear blackmail' three times, provoking Mao to plan the establishment of a nuclear weapons' programme.[3] Beijing's relationship with Moscow also soured in the latter half of the 1950s because of political and ideological reasons, especially, the widening gap between Mao and Khrushchev resulting in the development of the Sino-Soviet schism, which came to a head in the 1960s. The deteriorating geopolitical and regional security situation with respect to China, thus, demanded the setting up of an effective nuclear deterrence for which developing a robust and reliable ballistic missile capability as part of its delivery system was essential. The ballistic missile programme, thus established in 1956 also included within it a satellite programme, which initiated China's space activities. During its inception, the space programme was viewed as a medium for their larger ballistic missile programme rather than as a goal in itself.[4] It came into the forefront only after the Sputnik launch in 1957, when the military as well as the civilian benefits of space and satellite applications became clear to the Chinese government, including gaining technological prowess and international prestige for the nascent nation emerging after a century of backwardness and humiliation.[5] These contributed to the establishment of China's satellite programme.

China's space programme was kick-started by Qian Xuesen, widely acknowledged as the 'father of the nation's ballistic missile and space programme'. Qian had studied in the US, in prestigious technical institutes like the Massachusetts Institute of Technology (MIT) and the California Institute of Technology (Caltech). He had worked in the field of rocketry and had helped in setting up the Jet Propulsion Laboratories in the US. His proposals inspired the 1950's Dyna-Soar project, which ultimately led to the design of the Space Shuttle.[6] However, during the height of McCarthy witch hunts Qian, like certain other Chinese scientists and engineers working in the US, were accused of being a Communist and was deported to China in 1955. Beijing was quick to welcome him and others who were deported similarly from the US – Chen Fangyun (electronics expert), Sun Jiadong (rocket and satellite expert), Chen Kuanneng (metal physicist), Yang Jiaxi (automation specialist), Guo Yonghuai (aerodynamicist), and Wang Xiji (recoverable satellite specialist). China did so at a time when it badly required the technical resources required for setting up a robust science and technology base. Moreover, the initiation of the nuclear programme by Mao in 1955 created a pressing demand for the development of delivery systems. Qian himself made a proposal to the CPC Central Committee for establishing a national defence aeronautics industry in 1956. A Scientific Planning Commission was set up under the Premier Zhou Enlai after Mao's 1956 proposal to develop science and technology. It drew up a 'long range planning essentials for science and technology development, 1956-1957' for atomic energy, rockets, jet technology and computers. This led to the establishment of the 5th Research Academy of the Ministry of National Defence by the CPC Central Committee for the nation's space efforts on October 08, 1956, laying the official foundation of China's ballistic missile programme as well as its space programme. Qian was made the first director of the Rocket Research Institute established under the academy.[7]

Since China was lagging behind countries like the US and USSR in rocketry, it badly required outside technical assistance. This much-needed help was obtained from the Soviet Union through the signing of the 'New Defence Technical Accord' in October 1957.[8] However, this co-operation did not last long as the Sino-Soviet schism developed due to which the Soviets stopped all technical assistance in 1960. This resulted in China choosing a path towards indigenously developing its space programme with the initial Soviet technical know-how and the expertise of the US-returned team of scientists and engineers. The establishment and further growth of the programme would not have been possible without the state as well as military support when it came to technological as well as economic constraints.[9]

Table-2.1: Evolutionary Timeline of China's Space Programme

Year/Date	Milestone Events
October 08, 1956	Establishment of the 5th Academy of National Defence
October 1957	Signing of the New Defence Technical Accord with the Soviet Union
1958	Formation of group 581, initiating the satellite programme*
February 19, 1960	Launch of the first indigenous liquid fuelled rocket (T-7M)
1965	Restarting of the satellite programme
April 24, 1970	Launch of the first satellite (Dong Fang Hong-1) through the first Chang Zheng rocket (CZ-1)
1975	Launch and recovery of the first recoverable satellite (Fanhui Shi Weixing)
1979	The first ocean-going tracking ship (Yuanwang-1) commissioned
September 20, 1981	Three satellites launched on a single rocket for the first time (Shinjian-2, 2A, and 2B)
1986	Entry into the commercial launch programme
April 07, 1990	First commercial satellite launched (AsiaSat-1)
1992	Start of the manned space programme (Project 921 or the Shenzhou programme)
November 20, 1999	Launch of Shenzhou-1 (unmanned test flight)
October 14, 1999	Launch of the first China-Brazil Earth Resource Satellite (CBERS-1)
June 28, 2000	Launch of the first micro satellite (Tsinghua-1)
October 31, 2000	Launch of the first Beidou navigation satellite (Beidou-1)
October 15, 2003	Launch of the first manned spacecraft (Shenzhou-5)

April 18, 2004	Launch of the first nano satellite (Naxing-1)
September 27, 2008	First Extra Vehicular Activity in outer space (Shenzhou-7)
January 11, 2007	First ASAT test (on an own weather satellite)
October 24, 2007	Launch of the first unmanned lunar orbiter (Chang'e-1)
September 24, 2008	Launch of Tianlian-1, the first Data Relay Satellite (DRS)
end 2010	China matches with the US in number of space launches
October 02, 2011	First Space lab module launched (Tiangong-1)
November 02, 2011	Successful docking Shenzhou-8 of to Tiangong-1
end 2011	China surpasses the US in number of space launches

* The programme was shelved due to economic problems following the great famine in 1959

Notes

1. B. Harvey, *China's Space Program: From Conception to Manned Spaceflight* (UK: Praxis Publishing, 2004), pp. 15-17.
2. Ibid., p. 22.
3. R. Handberg and Z. Li, *Chinese Space Policy: A Study in Domestic and International Politics* (UK: Routledge, 2006), p. 64.
4. M. Midha, "Chinese Space Programme: Influence of Chinese Strategic Culture on its Development", *Air Power,* vol. 6, no. 1, Spring 2011, p. 79.
5. Ibid., p. 58.
6. E. Seedhouse, *The New Space Race: China v/s the United States,* (UK: Praxis Publishing, 2010), p. 14.
7. n. 1, pp. 20-22.
8. G. Kulaki and J.G. Lewis, *A Place for One's Mat: China's Space Program* (USA: American Academy of Arts and Sciences: 2009), p. 5.
9. n. 5.

3. The Infrastructure of China's Space Programme

The infrastructure of China's space programme consists of the organisation, launch facilities, the telemetry, tracking and control network and the launch vehicles. These facilities play a vital role in planning, enabling the launch of spacecrafts into orbits as well as controlling their orbital activities, thus, acting as the backbone of the space programme.

The Organisation

China's space programme was headed by the 5th Academy of National Defence for a period of about eight years – till 1964. Henceforth, the responsibility was transferred to the 7th Ministry of Machine Building until 1982, when the Ministry of Space Industry took over this responsibility.

In 1993, the Chinese National Space Administration (CNSA) was established, replacing the Ministry of Space Industry to take charge of China's space activities. This organisation is currently responsible for China's space activities to the Central Government through two different bodies. It is connected to the executive of the Central Government of China or the State Council through a body called the Space Leading Group, which was set up in 1991. This body consists of the Prime Minister, the Chairman of the Commission for Science, Technology and National Defence (COSTIND), the Vice Chairman of the State Committee for Science and Technology, the Minister of the Aerospace Industry, the Vice Minister of Foreign Affairs and the Vice Chairman of the State Committee for Central Planning. The CNSA is also responsible to the COSTIND, which directs China's scientific, research and industrial development.[1] All the activities of China's space programme is carried out by the executive arm of the CNSA, the China Aerospace Science and Technology Corporation (CASC), which was set up in 1989.

Fig. 3.1: Organisational Structure of China's Space Programme

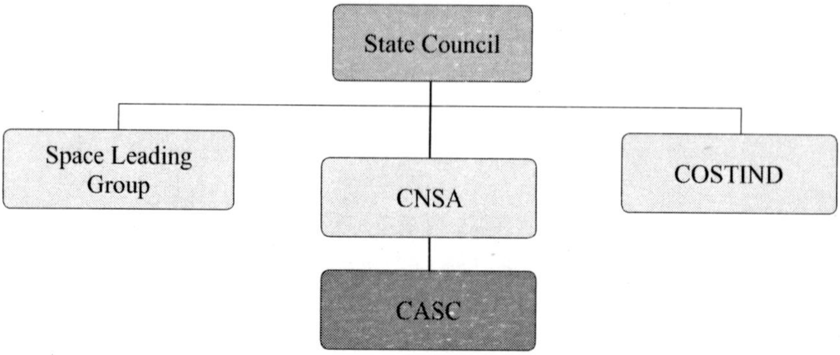

The CASC co-ordinates the constituents of the three main types of space organisational entities – 8 research and development as well as production bodies, 11 specialised companies, and 8 direct subordinate units.

Fig. 3.2: Organisation of CASC

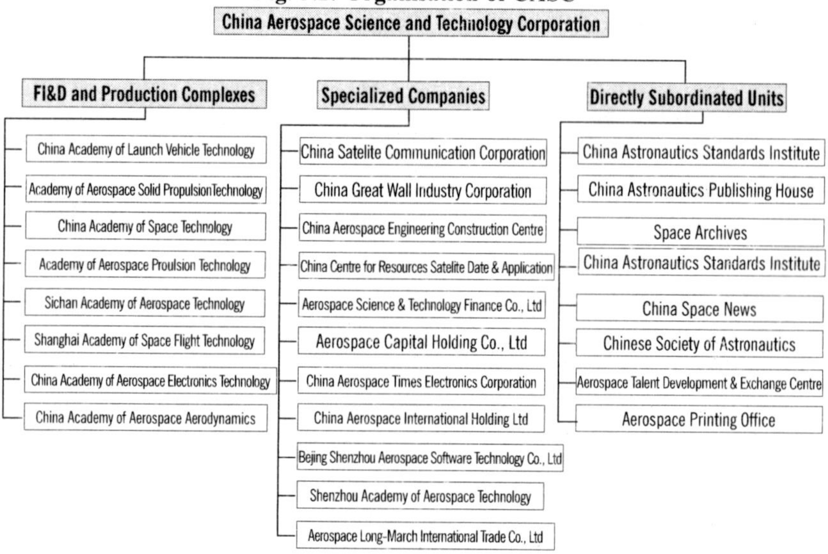

Source: CASC (http://www.spacechina.com/n16421/n17138/n17242/c127153/content.html)

Out of these entities of the CASC, 4 are of particular significance to China's space programme. Among these entities, 3 are research, development and production units. The Chinese Academy of Launch Vehicle Technology (CALT) was established in 1957, and is responsible for the Chang Zheng family of launch vehicles. The CALT has six factories distributed in both Beijing and Shanghai, with an overall capacity to manufacture almost 16 launch vehicles per year. These factories are connected to the launch sites through railways for transporting the launchers. The CALT also has facilities for static, vibration as well as engine tests. The China Academy for Space Technology (CAST) was established in 1968, and is responsible for the satellites and sounding rockets, and has three factories in Beijing where the satellites are manufactured. The Shanghai Academy of Space Flight Technology (SAST) was set up in 1961 so as to bring in the space industry into Shanghai. This academy has 13 factories and is responsible for the Chang Zheng-2D and Chang Zheng-4 types of launch vehicles, and also the guidance and altitude control systems of the Chang Zheng-3 vehicles. It is also responsible for the propulsion module, the electrical systems, the command and communications, and the main engine of the Shenzhou manned spacecraft. The China Great Wall Industry Corporation (CGWIC) is a specialised company under CASC and is its commercial marketing wing for the domestic and international space services market.[2]

Launch Centres

China has been setting up facilities for launching rockets into space since 1958. Up to now, three major space launch centres have been constructed for both domestic and international requirements at Jiuquan, Taiyuan and Xichang. The locations have been selected based on the geographical factors affecting launch effectiveness and economy, convenience of transportation as well as national security concerns; they are located inland. These facilities are claimed to have state-of-the-art facilities for launch vehicle and spacecraft testing, preparation, launch and in-flight tracking and safety control, as well as for orbit predictions.[3]

The first launch facility was established at Jiuquan and is called the Jiuquan Satellite Launch Centre (JSLC). It was established in 1958 as the first launch site for China's space programme.[4] It is located near the Gobi desert in Gansu province from where the manned missions, recoverable reconnaissance and earth resource satellites and sounding rockets are launched. The geographical coordinates of this launch site are 100°E and 41°N. Its location deep inland, which reduced its vulnerability from a US naval offensive, was a key security factor which figured in the selection of this site. The dry climate and extended hours of daylight which is characteristic of this arid region is highly favourable for space launches. The first rocket launch in 1960 and also the first satellite launch in 1970 took place from this centre.[5] It is used for launches into Low Earth Orbits (LEO) and Medium Earth Orbits (MEO) with large orbital inclination angles ranging from 40-56°. It now has the capability to assemble the rockets vertically.[6] This launch centre has so far carried out 49 launches out of which all except two were successful.

The second launch facility is the Taiyuan Satellite Launch Centre (TSLC), located in Taiyuan in the northern Shanxi province. It was established in 1966, was made operational in 1968, and used as a missile launch base. It is from this launch centre from which LEO and Sun-Synchronous Orbit (SSO) launches are conducted, especially of the weather, earth observation and scientific satellites.[7] This centre could be used for launching satellites in both LEO and MEO.[8] The geographical co-ordinates of this launch site are 37°30'N 112°36'E. The dry climate here, too, facilitates launches. The initial space launch was carried out here in 1988 when the first meteorological satellite was launched. This launch centre has so far carried out 36 launches which were all successful.

The third launch facility is the Xichang Satellite Launch Centre (XSLC) located at Xichang in the southern Sichuan province. It was established in 1970 and made operational in 1984. The geographical co-ordinates of this launch site are 28°12'N 102°02'E and are, thus, located closest to the equator. Its location was also preferred as it was far from the coast and the northern borders, which reduced the risk of a possible attack from the US and the USSR respectively.[9] XSLC is China's only low-latitude launch site, capable of launching at inclinations ranging from 28-36°. It is therefore used for geostationary launches, primarily for communication, broadcasting and meteorological satellites. It is also used for launching powerful thrust rockets, and is the only site in China for launching international commercial missions. Launches are done ideally during the period October to May when the weather conditions are favourable.[10] This launch centre has so far carried out 70 launches out of which 6 have failed.

Telemetry, Tracking and Control (TT&C) Facilities

A TT&C network has been developed by China for controlling its assets in space as well as for assisting the launch and recovery process. This network, along with the launch centres is managed by an organisation called the China Satellite Launch and Tracking Control General (CLTC) working under the COSTIND.[11] China's first TT&C network was established in the late 1960s and became operational in the early 1970s. They were further expanded to cover both the domestic as well as international space operations since the establishment of the commercial launch programme in the 1980s.[12] This network is also used for the ballistic missile programme and therefore forms a vital part of the national defence infrastructure. The TT&C network comprises of ground command and control centres and tracking stations, tracking ships and a Data Relay Satellite (DRS) system in orbit.

The ground facilities consists of the Beijing Aerospace Command and Control Centre (BACC) in Beijing Aerospace City, the Xi'an Satellite Control Centre (XSCC) in Shaanxi province, and 13 land-based space tracking stations out of which 10 are within and 3 outside China. The BACC is the primary command and control centre for the manned as well as the lunar and deep space exploration missions.[13] The XSCC located at Weinan, near Xi'an is the primary satellite control facility in China. The tracking stations within the Chinese territory are at Weinan in Shaanxi province, Changchun in Jilin province, Qingdao in Shandong province, Zhanyi in Yunnan province, Nanhai in Hainan island, Kashi in Xinjiang autonomous region, Xiamen in Fujian province, Lushan in Jianxi province, Jiamusi in Heilongjiang province, and Dongfeng in Inner Mongolia autonomous region along with mobile tracking stations in the Xinjiang and Inner Mongolia autonomous regions. The overseas tracking stations are located at Karachi in Pakistan, Malindi in Kenya, and Swakopmund in Namibia, which came up primarily to support the manned space programme. In addition to these, agreements have been made with France, Brazil, Sweden and Australia for the sharing of space tracking facilities. China has also deployed six Yuanwang (or Long View) class space tracking ships starting from the late 1970s for supplementing the land based tracking systems. They are positioned at the Western Pacific, the Southern Pacific, the Southern Atlantic and the Indian Oceans.[14] To complement these land and sea facilities, two Tianlian series of satellites have been launched for tracking and data relay purposes, which would reduce China's reliance on the foreign tracking stations.[15]

Fig. 3.3: Map of Space Launch and TT&C Facilities Within China

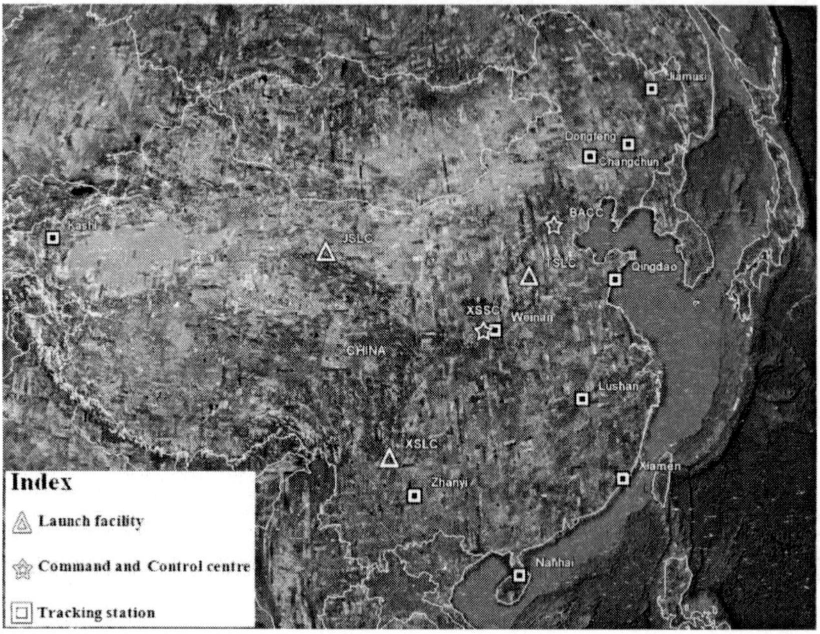

Launch Vehicles

The launch vehicles for China's space applications were derived from its ballistic missiles. During the initial years of China's ballistic missile programme in the late 1950s, China acquired the R-1 and R-2 ballistic missiles from the Soviet Union to develop the first Chinese missiles. The Soviets also supplied the necessary technical expertise, design documentation and the tooling for production. After the Soviet Union's withdrawal from the co-operation agreement in 1960, China went on to develop its own version of the R-2, called the Dong Feng-1 (DF-1) short range ballistic missile. It was followed in the 1960s by the first indigenously developed ballistic missile, the medium range Dong Feng-2 (DF-2) and the DF-3 and DF-4 intermediate range ballistic missiles.

The DF-4 was modified as China's first launch vehicle to carry the nation's first satellite into the LEO in 1970, becoming the 5th nation capable of orbital launch. [16] This became the first Chang Zheng (CZ) or Long March carrier rocket, the CZ-1. It was named after Mao's historic Long March of the 1930s and had two liquid propellant stages and a third stage fuelled by solid propellants. Similarly, the first Chinese intercontinental ballistic missile, the DF-5 which was successfully tested in 1971, was modified into the two stage CZ-2.[17] The CZ series further expanded with many variants of CZ-2. The CZ-2C/SD (Smart Dispenser) was a variant developed with an additional third stage fuelled by solid propellants for launching the Iridium global wireless communications satellite network. The CZ-2F version was developed especially for the manned space programme and was fitted with four strap-on boosters and an emergency escape system. The CZ-2 series is now primarily used for LEO and Geostationary Transfer Orbit (GTO) missions. This was followed by the development of the three-stage CZ-3 in which a cryogenic engine was introduced at the upper stage providing re-start capability, which allows heavier payloads to be launched to GTO, its intended destination. The CZ-3B in this category is the most powerful among the CZ family and is used for launching heavy satellites, having four strap-on boosters introduced in its first stage. The CZ-3C, which was developed later, had only two boosters suitable for launching smaller satellites, and therefore, making the launch vehicle family more versatile. In addition to these, the CZ-4 rockets were developed to be used as back-up to the CZ-3 series. However, currently the CZ-4 series launch vehicles are intended for launches to SSO. In total, China has developed 12 types of CZ launch vehicles, out of which currently only 8 are operational.[18] China has been developing the capabilities to carry out launches mostly to the key LEO, SSO and GTO orbits. This has helped it to pursue space projects for diverse applications. As on end 2011, 62 launches have been carried out to LEO, 1 to MEO (Middle Earth Orbit), 29 to SSO and 55 to GTO. In total, China has carried out a total of 147 successful launches through its CZ carrier rockets with a success rate of 95 per cent, (8 launches were failures).

Table-3.1: Currently Operational Launch Vehicles

Launch Vehicle	L/D* Mass Stages	First flight	Missions	Launch sites	Launch capability (kg)			Success
					LEO*	SSO	GTO	
CZ-2C	43 m / 3.35 m 233T 3 stage	1975	Remote Sensing Scientific Communication Commercial	JSLC TSLC XLSC	3,850	2,100	1,250	35/36 (97%)
CZ-2D	41 m / 3.80 m 250 T 2 stage	1992	Communication Remote Sensing	JSLC	4,000	1,150		15/15 (100%)
CZ-2F	58.30 m 498 T 2 stage	1999	Manned spaceflight	JSLC	8,600			9/9 (100%)

CZ-3A	52.52 m / 3.35 m 241 T 3 stage	1994	Communication Navigation Meteorology Lunar probe	XSLC			2,600	22/22 (100%)
CZ-3B	56.33 m / 4.20 m 456 T 3 stage	1996	Communication Commercial	XSLC			5,500	17/18 (94%)
CZ-3C	54.84 m / 4 m 345 T 3 stage	2008	Navigation Lunar probe	XLSC			3,800	7/7 (100%)
CZ-4B	48 m / 3.80 m 250 T 3 stage	1999	Scientific Meteorology Remote Sensing	JSLC TSLC		2,230		16/16 (100%)
CZ-4C	48 m / 3.80 m 250 T 3 stage	2006	Remote Sensing Meteorology	JSLC TSLC		2,950		7/7 (100%)

* L/D – Total length/Maximum faring diameter

Fig. 3.4: The Chang Zheng Family of Launch Vehicles

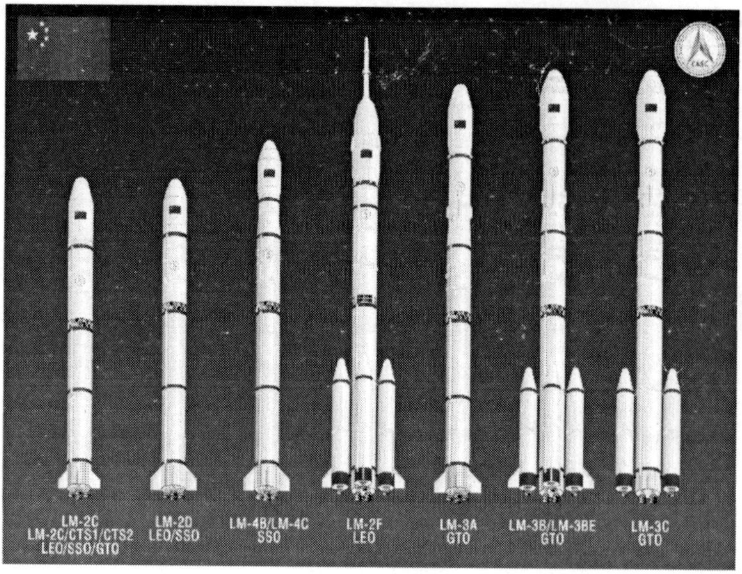

Source: The China Great Wall Industry Corporation (www.cgwic.com)

Fig. 3.5: China's Trends in Space Launches (1970-2011) and GDP (1970-2010)

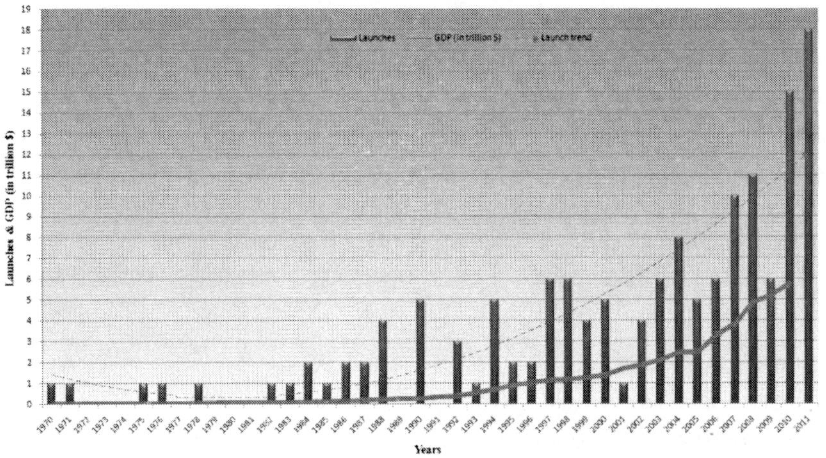

Analysing the launch trend, it could be observed that there has been an initial lull in space launches. Thus, the launch frequency gathered considerable momentum only after the mid-1980s. Further, the launch rate accelerated through the 21st century, with growing diversity in the projects pursued like the manned spaceflight, navigation as well as the lunar exploration programmes. During the initial decade of the 1970s, the number of launches was only 5. This increased in the 1980s to 13, by the 1990s to 34 and by the 2000s to 76, with the launches doubling every decade. On a long term average, China has been carrying out a launch every 3 to 4 months, with a rate of about 3 to 4 launches per year. In 2010, China carried out a record 15 space launches, matching that of the US for first time.[19] This was followed by China's with 18 launches in 2011 overtaking the US by one launch.[20] These facts reflect on the increasing launch capacity and infrastructure of the nation's space programme. This is also a reflection on the level of support and emphasis being given to the space programme by the government. The trend in China's space activity is also very much in consonance with the rise in its economic power[21] as could be observed from the above figure.

Apart from the CZ series of conventional liquid propellant launch vehicles, China has also developed the Kaituozhe (or Explorer) series of solid propellant launch vehicles since 2000, which are based on the DF-31 solid propellant ICBM.[22] The Kaituozhe-1 (KT-1) is capable of launching up to 50 kg payload to LEO. It has a four stage design, and can be launched from a mobile launch facility. It is reported that two launches have been attempted in 2002 and 2003 without success. This rocket was supposedly used as a kinetic-kill vehicle in the ASAT test conducted on January 11, 2007 to bring down the old inactive Fengyun-1C meteorological satellite. Improved variants have been developed called the KT-1A and the KT-1B. The KT-1A is capable of launching up to 300 kg payload to GTO and polar orbits, and the KT-1B is capable of launching up to 400 kg to polar orbits.[23] These could be used to launch small satellites, an emerging trend in China's satellite programme.

Notes

1. n. 1, pp. 170-171.
2. Ibid., pp. 171-175.
3. The China Great Wall Industrial Corporation, "Launch Sites", see http://www.cgwic.com/LaunchServices/LaunchSite/JSLC.html, accessed on June 14, 2011.
4. L. Ge and Z. Yao, "Following an Indigenous Path: China's Space Activities from 1956 to 2006", in P.V. Manoranjan Rao (ed.), *50 Years of Space: A Global Perspective* (Hyderabad: Universities Press (India) Private Limited, 2007), p. 186.
5. "China's Three Major Space Launch Bases", *The China Daily*, October 15, 2003, see http://www.chinadaily.com.cn/en/doc/2003-10/15/content_272334.htm, accessed on June 14, 2011.
6. L. Zhi, "Backgrounder: China's Four Space Launch Bases", *Xinhua News Agency*, January 10, 2010, see http://news.xinhuanet.com/english2010/database/2010-01/10/c_13131894.htm, accessed on June 14, 2011.
7. M.S. Smith, "China's Space Program: An Overview", *CRS Report for Congress*, October 18, 2005, pp. 1-2, see www.fas.org/sgp/crs/space/RS21641.pdf, accessed on February 10, 2011.
8. n. 15.
9. n. 3, p. 65.
10. "China's Satellite Launch Centers", *The China Daily*, September 23, 2008, see http://www.chinadaily.com.cn/china/2008-09/23/content_7052063.htm, accessed on June 14, 2011.
11. "China Satellite Launch and Tracking General [CLTC]", see http://www.fas.org/nuke/guide/china/contractor/cltc.htm, accessed on June 15, 2011.
12. W. Long, "China Builds Advanced Spacecraft Tracking and Command Network", May 29, 2000, see http://www.spacedaily.com/news/china-00za.html, accessed on June 15, 2011.

13. "Beijing Aerospace Command & Control Centre", December 01, 2010, see http://www.sinodefence.com/space/facility/bacc.asp, accessed on June 15, 2011.
14. "Tracking, Telemetry & Command (TT&C) Network", see http://www.sinodefence.com/space/facility/space-ttc.asp, accessed on June 15, 2011.
15. S. Clark, "Chinese Data Relay Spacecraft Put into Orbit", see http://www.spaceflightnow.com/news/n0804/25tianlian1/, accessed on June 16, 2011.
16. S.J. Isakowitz, Joshua B. Hopkins and Joseph P. Hopkins Jr., *International Reference Guide to Space Launch Systems* (USA: American Institute of Aeronautics and Astronautics, 2004), pp. 261-262.
17. K. Lalitendra, "Dragon in Space: Implications for India", *Air Power*, vol. 3, no. 3, Monsoon 2008, p. 68.
18. All launch vehicle details are obtained from the China Great Wall Industrial Corporation website, see http://www.cgwic.com , accessed on June 22, 2011.
19. D. Axe, "China Matches US Space Launches for First Time", December 23, 2010, see http://www.wired.com/dangerroom/2010/12/china-matches-u-s-space-launches-for-first-time/,
20. S. Clark, "China Lofts New Satellite, Breaks US Rocket Launch Record", see http://www.space.com/14048-china-satellite-launch-breaks-rocket record.html?utm_source=feedburner&utm_medium=feed&utm_campaign=Feed%3A+spaceheadlines+%28SPACE.com+Headline+Feed%29, accessed on February 10, 2012.
21. China's GDP records available at http://www.chinability.com/GDP.htm, accessed on July 24, 2011.
22. n. 25, p. 204.
23. "Kaituozhe 1 (KT-1) Launch Vehicle", February 20, 2009, see http://www.sinodefence.com/space/launcher/kaituozhe1.asp, accessed on June 23, 2011.

4. China's Space Missions

China's missions in space include its satellite, the human spaceflight and the space exploration programmes. Of these, satellite programme is the most significant because of the role satellites play in modernising the nation and augmenting its security and development. The human spaceflight programme's relevance is in its symbolism of the nation's greatness as well the manned exploration of space. The space exploration programme mostly focuses on the lunar and Martian exploration, with the component of human spaceflight coming in its later stages for the purpose of manned space exploration. Achievements in these areas highlight the scientific and technological prowess of the nation, and give it an edge in dealing with geopolitical challenges. Of these programmes, the satellite component is at its advanced stage, while the other two sectors are still evolving, albeit with major breakthroughs.

The Satellite Programme

China's first satellite launch took place in 1970, with the Dong Fang Hong-1 (The East is Red) telecommunication satellite, and thus, became the 5th nation to do so. It orbited the earth for 26 days transmitting the revolutionary Chinese song 'The East is Red'. This marked the first major milestone of China's odyssey into outer space and establishing its presence there. Since then, several other types of satellites were developed by the Chinese for diverse requirements. The four main areas of application of China's satellite programme are Remote Sensing, Telecommunications, Navigation, and Scientific exploration. As on end 2011, there are 82 active Chinese satellites in orbit. Out of these, 33 are remote sensing (out of which 5 are meteorological), 17 are telecommunication, 12 are navigation and 20 are scientific exploration satellites. Among these, 20 satellites are distributed in LEO, 1 in MEO, 31 in SSO, 5 in IGSO (Inclined Geo Synchronous Orbit), 24 in GEO (Geostationary Earth Orbit), and 1 in HEO (Highly Elliptical Orbit).[1]

Remote Sensing

The satellites developed for remote sensing are officially stated to be used for earth monitoring applications including meteorology, cartography, mining, agriculture, forestry, hydrology, oceanography, seismology, environmental protection, disaster mitigation and urban planning.[2] However, this has given China a space-based image collection capability, which could also be used for military reconnaissance purposes.

For meteorological applications, China has developed the Fengyun (Wind and Cloud/FY) series of satellites. Three categories of these satellites have been launched by China since the first Fengyun satellite (FY-1) took off in 1988. The FY-1 and FY-3 are meant for conducting global meteorological observations in the SSOs, while the FY-2 is a geostationary meteorological satellite which monitors China and its neighbouring regions. The FY-1 and the FY-2 satellites are of the optical and Infra Red imaging type whereas the FY-3 satellites are of the multi-spectral imaging type.[3] The launches of FY-2D and FY-2E satellites on December 2006 and May 2008 respectively were also intended to cater to the critical weather forecasting requirements during the 2008 Beijing Olympics, and have thus helped China to organise successfully the major international event. Apart from being part of the China Meteorological Administration (CMA), Fengyun-1 and 2 satellites are also included in the WMO's Global Observing System satellites.[4] Currently, 5 Fengyun satellites are active in orbit, providing global coverage and having a maximum imaging resolution of 250 m.

The Ziyuan (Resources/ZY) satellite series is a much debated over satellite series as its details are not disclosed in the public domain except for the officially stated purpose that these are used for land resource monitoring purposes. Therefore it has been presumed by outside observers that they are dedicated military reconnaissance satellites, part of the military's 'Jian Bing' class of satellites.[5] Currently there are 3 Ziyuan satellites which are active in the orbit. These satellites are in the SSOs, which gives them a global coverage. The ZY-1(02C) has a maximum resolution of 2.36 m, the highest declared satellite resolution by China. The remote sensing/reconnaissance satellites of the recoverable type, the Fanhui Shi Weixing series, appears to have concluded in 2006 as all satellites launched have been recovered and no further launches have taken place. Since then, China has launched a new family of satellites called the Yaogan (Remote Sensing/YG) series. These are again remote sensing satellites for civilian applications like land resource observations as stated by China whose details are not disclosed, and is, thus, being considered as military-oriented satellites. Currently, there are fourteen Yaogan satellites active in orbit, from Yaogan-2 to Yaogan 11. Yaogan-9A, 9B and 9C operate as a three-satellite constellation in the 63.4° orbit with individual orbit period of 107.1 minutes.

This would reduce the effective orbit period of the constellation to half an hour, and therefore changes in very short intervals of time can be monitored. Yaogan-3, 6, 8 and 10 are understood to be Synthetic Aperture Radar (SAR) capable satellites.[6] This appears so, especially considering the fact that only these satellites have been developed by the SAST, while the others of the electro-optical variety are developed by CAST. SAR is not included in the officially stated list of payload instruments that CAST has developed[7], which could be existing in the case of SAST.

China has been increasingly been concentrating on developing small satellites and launching them into SSO for the purposes of remote sensing and possibly reconnaissance. The advantage of small satellites is that they allow rapid expansion as well as replacement of the existing satellite force, especially during instances when there are critical service disruptions.[8] In 1998, the Tsinghua University of China reached a research co-operation agreement with the University of Surrey, UK on micro satellites. As a result, in May 2000, there was a successful launch of a micro satellite called Tsinghua-1. The Beijing (BJ) satellite (Tsinghua-2), which is currently in orbit, was launched from the Plesetsk mobile launch facility in Russia in 2005 and was meant for disaster monitoring as well as Olympics planning. The three Chuangxin (Innovation/CX) micro satellites launched in 2003, 2008 and 2011 are also meant for environment as well as disaster monitoring purposes. China has extended its remote sensing capability to the oceans by launching the Haiyang (Ocean/HY) series of small satellites, which is capable of providing a resolution of 250 m.[9] The first satellite was launched in 2002. The second and the third satellite, launched in 2007 and 2011 respectively, are currently active in the orbit. The launch of these satellites comes at a time when China is trying to increase its influence over the seas, not only in the Western Pacific, but also in the Indian Ocean as result of its growing economic and security interests in these regions. Two Tansuo or Shiyuan (Experiment/TS or SY) mini satellites were launched by China since 2004 for land resources and atmospheric observation on an experimental basis. These were jointly developed by the Harbin Polytechnic University, Chinese Research Institute of Space Technology in Changchun, Chinese Academy of Sciences (CAS) and Xi'an Surveys and Designs Institute. The Shiyuan-1, which was launched in 2004, is China's first satellite capable of 3D imaging. China has also launched a constellation of two small satellites in 2008, called the Huanjing (Environment/HJ) series for the purpose of environment and disaster monitoring. These satellites are in the 97.95° SSO, which provides global coverage, and also has a maximum resolution of 30 m. The latest addition in China's remote sensing satellites in orbit is the Tianhui (Mapping/TH) satellite. It is a new type of small satellite launched into SSO by China in 2010, which is capable of 3D mapping as well as having a maximum resolution of 5 m, and was developed by the China Spacesat Co. Ltd.

Table-4.1: Existing Remote Sensing Satellites

Satellite	Purpose	Launch Centre	Launch Vehicle	Launch Date	Orbit	Position	Remarks
FY-1D	Meteorology	TSLC	CZ-4B	May 15, 2002	SSO	98.71°	Optical/IR imaging 1100m resolution
FY-2D		XSLC	CZ-3A	December 08, 2006	GEO	86.5° E	Optical/IR imaging 1250 m resolution
FY-3A		TSLC	CZ-4C	May 27, 2008	SSO	98.69°	Multispectral imaging 250 m resolution
FY-2E		XSLC	CZ-3A	December 23, 2008	GEO	105° E	Optical/IR imaging 1250 m resolution
FY-3B		TSLC	CZ-4C	November 05, 2010	SSO	98.72°	Multispectral imaging 250 m resolution
YG-2	Earth observation	JSLC	CZ-2D	May 25, 2007	LEO	97.8°	Electro-optical imagery (CAST)
YG-3		TSLC	CZ-4C	November 12, 2007	SSO	97.85°	SAR imagery (SAST)

YG-4	Earth observation	JSLC	CZ-2D	December 01, 2008	LEO	97.83°	Electro-optical imagery (CAST)
YG-5		TSLC	CZ-4B	December 15, 2008	LEO	97.3°	Electro-optical imagery (CAST)
YG-6		TSLC	CZ-2C	April 22, 2009	SSO	97.56°	SAR imagery (SAST)
YG-7		JSLC	CZ-2D	December 09, 2009	LEO	97.92°	Electro-optical imagery (CAST)
YG-8		TSLC	CZ-4C	December 15, 2009	LEO	100.5°	SAR imagery (SAST)
YG-9A		JSLC	CZ-4C	March 05, 2010	LEO	63.4°	Electro-optical imagery (CAST)
YG-9B		JSLC	CZ-4C	March 05, 2010	LEO	63.4°	Electro-optical imagery (CAST)
YG-9C		JSLC	CZ-4C	March 05, 2010	LEO	63.4°	Electro-optical imagery (CAST)
YG-10		TSLC	CZ-4C	August 10, 2010	SSO	97.83°	SAR imagery (SAST)
YG-11		JSLC	CZ-2D	September 22, 2010	SSO	98°	Electro-optical imagery (CAST)
YG-12		TSLC	CZ-4B	November 09, 2011	LEO	97.4°	
YG-13		TSLC	CZ-2C	November 30, 2011	LEO	97.1 °	
ZY-2B	Land resource observation	TSLC	CZ-4B	October 27, 2002	SSO	97.1°	Dedicated military satellite
ZY-2C		TSLC	CZ-4B	November 06, 2004	SSO	97.3°	
ZY-1(02C)		TSLC	CZ-4B	December 22, 2011	SSO	98.5 °	2.36 m
HJ-1A	Environment and disaster monitoring	TSLC	CZ-2C	September 06, 2008	SSO	97.95°	30 m resolution
HJ-1B		TSLC	CZ-2C	September 06, 2008	SSO	97.95°	
HY-1B	Ocean monitoring	TSLC	CZ-2C	April 11, 2007	SSO	98.46°	250 m resolution
HY-2		TSLC	CZ-4B	August 16, 2011	SSO	99.4°	

TH-1	Mapping	JSLC	CZ-2D	August 24, 2010	SSO	97.37°	5 m resolution
BJ-1	Imaging	Plesetsk (Russia)	Cosmos-3M	October 27, 2005	SSO	98°	4 m resolution
TS-1 (SY-1)	Earth observation	XSLC	CZ-2C	April 18, 2004	SSO	97.45°	1st 3D imaging satellite 10 m resolution
TS-2 (SY-2)		XSLC	CZ-2C	November 18, 2004	LEO	98.1°	3D imaging satellite
CX-1(1)	Environment and disaster monitoring	TSLC	CZ-4B	October 21, 2003	SSO	98.5°	Micro satellites
CX-1(2)		JSLC	CZ-2D	November 05, 2008	LEO	98.47°	
CX-1(3)		TSLC	CZ-2D	November 20, 2011	LEO	98.5 °	

Telecommunication and Broadcasting

The very first satellite launched into orbit by China in 1970 was a telecommunications satellite. China has currently four types of telecommunications satellites active in the orbit. The Zhongxing (China Star/ZX) series is the state owned telecommunications satellite, AP Star is a commercial satellite of the APT Corporation based in Hong Kong, Tianlian (Sky Link/TL) is a tracking and data relay satellite, and Xiwang (Hope/XW) is an amateur radio micro satellite made for the youth. There are currently three AP Star satellites, eleven Zhongxing and two Tianlian satellites in GEO, and one Xiwang satellite in LEO.

The AP Star satellite is entirely based on foreign satellite bus, namely the FS1300 and the SB4000C2 of Space Systems/Loral (US) and the Thales Alenia Space (France) respectively. Meanwhile, the Zhongxing satellites buses are mainly from the indigenous Dong Fang Hong (DFH) series of satellite system – the DFH-3 and the DFH-4. However, they also use foreign made satellite buses like the A2100A from Lockheed Martin (US), SB3000 from Aerospatiale (France) and SB4000 from Thales Alenia Space. The Tianlian satellite is exclusively based on the DFH-3 bus.

In terms of coverage, the AP Star-2R has the largest area of coverage including almost the entire Eurasia as well as parts of Africa and Oceania. Among the Zhongxing satellites, the Zhongxing 6B has the maximum coverage area including the whole of Asian continent and Oceania, and Zhongxing-9 has the least coverage area, limited to China and its immediate neighbourhood. The remaining AP Star satellites and Zhongxing satellites have regional coverage over the Asia Pacific.[10] The Tianlian satellites, which were put into orbit to facilitate communication between the China's spacecrafts and the ground stations have increased the coverage area of tracking from a mere 15 per cent using only the ground facilities to almost half of the spacecraft's trajectory.

Fig. 4.1: Coverage of Various Chinese Telecommunication Satellites

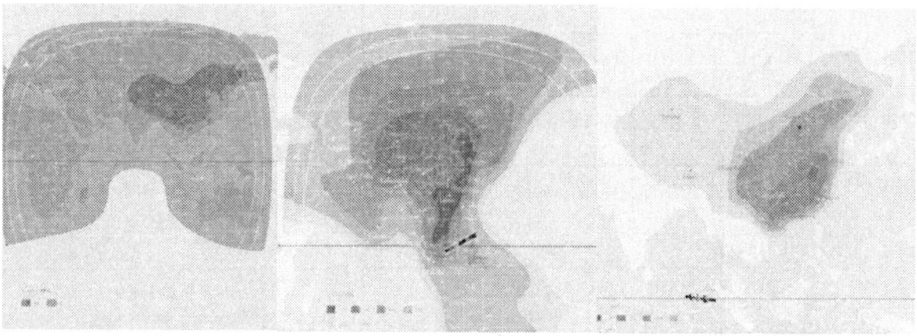

AP Star-2R   Zhongxing-6B   Zhongxing-9

Source: China Satellite Communications Co. Ltd. (www.chinasatcom.com)

There have been speculations about Zhongxing-20, 20A, 22A and 1A satellites as being dedicated military communication satellites under the names Shentong (Zhongxing-20), Fenghuo 1 (Zhongxing 22), Fenghuo 1-02 (Zhongxing 22A) and Fenghuo 2 (Zhongxing 1A).[11] This appears to be actually so as there is very little information officially declared on these satellites. Further, these satellites are not mentioned in the list of satellites operated by the state owned China Satellite Communications Co. Ltd. which operates all the other Zhongxing satellites.[12] Since all three of these satellites have been based on the indigenous DFH-3 platform, comparing their weight with other DFH-3 satellites of the same series, the number of transponders can be roughly estimated to be around 10 to 11 in each of these satellites. Considering this, the number of existing Chinese transponders could be well over 400.

Table-4.2: Existing Telecommunication Satellites

Satellite	Launch Centre	Launch Vehicle	Launch Date	Orbit	Position	Remarks
ZX-5A	XSLC	CZ-3B	May 30, 1998	GEO	87.5°E	18 C and 20 Ku-band transponders Regional coverage
ZX-5B	XSLC	CZ-3B	July 18, 1998	GEO	110.5°E	24 C and 14 Ku-band transponders Regional coverage
ZX-20	XSLC	CZ-3A	November 15, 2003	GEO	98.17° E	10 transponders
ZX-22A	XSLC	CZ-3A	September 13, 2006	GEO	98° E	10 transponders
ZX-5C	XSLC	CZ-3A	June 01, 2007	GEO	125° E	10 C-band transponders Regional coverage
ZX-6B	XSLC	CZ-3B	July 05, 2007	GEO	115.5°E	38 C-band transponders Continental coverage
ZX-9	XSLC	CZ-3B	June 09, 2008	GEO	92.2° E	22 Ku-band transponders National coverage
ZX-6A	XSLC	CZ-3B	June 05, 2010	GEO	125°E	1 S, 24 C and 8 Ku-band transponders Regional coverage
ZX-20A	XSLC	CZ-3A	November 25, 2010	GEO	130°E	20 transponders
ZX-10	XSLC	CZ-3B	June 20, 2011	GEO	110.5°E	30 C and 16 Ku-band transponders Regional coverage
ZX-1A	XSLC	CZ-3B	September 17, 2011	GEO	129.7° E	20 transponders
APStar-2R	XSLC	CZ-3B	October 17, 1997	GEO	76.5°E	28 C and 15 Ku-band transponders Semi-global coverage
APStar-5	Sea Launch	Zenit 3SL	June 29, 2004	GEO	138°E	38 C and 16 Ku-band transponders Regional coverage
APStar-6	XSLC	CZ-3B	December 04, 2005	GEO	134°E	38 C and 12 Ku-band transponders Regional coverage
TL-1(1)	XSLC	CZ-3C	April 25, 2008	GEO	77° E	Tracking and data relay service
TL-1(2)	XSLC	CZ-3C	July 11, 2011	GEO	176.7°E	
XW-1	TSLC	CZ-4C	December 15, 2009	LEO	100.4°	Amateur radio micro satellite

Navigation

China has become the third nation to develop Beidou (Compass/BD), its own global satellite navigation system after GPS (US) and GLONASS (Russia). It will be the 4th such international project after GPS, GLONASS and Galileo (Europe). This system has its roots in the 1980s, and took on the shape of the Beidou experimental satellite navigation system in 2000 when the first geostationary satellite for the purpose was launched. It was followed by three more satellites, setting up the first experimental phase of the network. From 2007, the second phase, started under which 5 geostationary and 30 non-geostationary satellites, were to be put into the orbit, to establish a regional satellite navigation system by 2012 and further extension into a global system by 2020. It is developed by CAST and offers to provide an accuracy of 10 m for location and 0.2 m/s for velocity. It is also stated to be compatible and interoperable with the other existing satellite navigation systems. With the initial phase of the system in place, China claims to benefit from it as in the case of the 2008 Olympics as well as the disaster relief operations during the Wenchuan and Yushu earthquakes of 2008 and 2010 respectively.[13]

The development of such a programme can be seen as China's efforts to achieve self-reliance in high accuracy navigation and positioning, avoiding any kind of dependence on foreign systems. Currently, there are only 2 active satellites remaining from the first phase, and 10 from the second phase out of which 4 are in GEO, and the remaining 6 are in non-GEO orbits (1 in MEO and 5 in IGSO).

Table-4.3: Existing Navigation Satellites

Satellite	Launch Centre	Launch Vehicle	Launch Date	Orbit	Position
BD-1B	XSLC	CZ-3A	December 21, 2000	GEO	80.6° E
BD-1C	XSLC	CZ-3A	May 25, 2003	GEO	110.6° E
BD-M1	XSLC	CZ-3A	April 14, 2007	MEO	56.5°
BD-G2	XSLC	CZ-3C	April 15, 2009	GEO	120° E
BD-G1	XSLC	CZ-3C	January 17, 2010	GEO	141.5° E
BD-G3	XSLC	CZ-3C	June 02, 2010	GEO	84.6°E
BD-IGSO(1)	XSLC	CZ-3A	August 01, 2010	IGSO	54.9°
BD-G4	XSLC	CZ-3C	November 01, 2010	GEO	160.1° E
BD-IGSO(2)	XSLC	CZ-3A	December 18, 2010	IGSO	55.1°
BD-IGSO(3)	XSLC	CZ-3A	April 09, 2011	IGSO	55.4°
BD-IGSO(4)	XSLC	CZ-3A	July 27, 2011	IGSO	55.2°
BD-IGSO(5)	XSLC	CZ-3A	December 02, 2011	IGSO	55.1 °

Scientific Exploration

The Shijian (Practice/SJ) series of satellites are the most prominent among the scientific exploration satellites developed by China meant for studying the space environment as well as conducting scientific experiments and technological tests. Currently there are 13 active satellites in orbit out of which 10 are in SSO and 3 are in LEO. The types of payload in these satellites mostly include particle detectors and field detectors which study the space environment, as well as systems dealing with testing new space technologies and scientific experiments in zero-gravity conditions. Launch of these satellites started gaining momentum only during the latter half of the last decade, considering the fact that prior to that only six such satellites have been launched. Therefore, it could be inferred that during the past 5 years, a comparatively high amount of testing of new technologies have been taking place. This obviously points to the rapid pace at which Chinese space research and development capabilities are growing.

China has developed a mini satellite series called Tance (Probe/TC) jointly with Europe for the first time as part of the 'Double Star' project for the purpose of probing and predicting geomagnetic storms, which is one of the major factors causing disruptions in satellite operations. The agreement for joint development of these satellites was made in 2001 between the CNSA and the European Space Agency (ESA). According to this, two Chinese satellites will be operating along with four European satellites in regions of space that have not been covered by other satellites. The first satellite launched in 2003 was an equatorial orbiting probe put in a HEO with an apogee double that of GEO, becoming the highest orbiting satellite China has ever launched. The second satellite, which is still active, is a polar orbiting probe and was launched in 2004. The third and fourth Shiyuan mini satellites were designed for experimenting with space technologies and environment probing, unlike its predecessors which were used in remote sensing. The Tianxun is a micro satellite launched in 2011, which was designed by the Nanjing Institute of Aeronautics and Astronautics for technological verification tests.

In addition to these mini and micro satellites, China has also developed nano and pico satellites, which are active in the orbit. The Naxing (Nano satellite/NX) is the first nano satellite developed by China, for the purpose of testing new satellite technologies. This satellite was developed jointly by the Tsinghua University and the Aerospace Tsinghua Satellite Technologies Co. Ltd. The Zheda Pixing (Zhejiang pico satellite/ZP) series are pico satellites developed by the Zhejiang University for microelectronics studies, with currently two satellites operating in orbit.[14]

Table-4.4: Existing Scientific Exploration Satellites

Satellite	Launch Centre	Launch Vehicle	Launch Date	Orbit	Position
SJ-6A	TSLC	CZ-4B	September 08, 2004	SSO	97.8°
SJ-6B	TSLC	CZ-4B	September 08, 2004	SSO	97.8°
SJ-7	JSLC	CZ-2D	July 06, 2005	SSO	97.7°
SJ-6C	TSLC	CZ-4B	October 24, 2006	SSO	97.7°
SJ-6D	TSLC	CZ-4B	October 24, 2006	SSO	97.7°
SJ-6E	TSLC	CZ-4B	October 25, 2006	SSO	97.6°
SJ-6F	TSLC	CZ-4B	October 25, 2006	SSO	97.6°
SJ-11(1)	JSLC	CZ-2C	September 12, 2004	SSO	98.2°
SJ-12	JSLC	CZ-2D	June 15, 2010	LEO	97.7°
SJ-6G	TSLC	CZ-4B	October 06, 2006	LEO	97.7°
SJ-6H	TSLC	CZ-4B	October 06, 2006	LEO	97.7°
SJ-11(3)	JSLC	CZ-2C	July 06, 2011	SSO	98.2°
SJ-11(2)	JSLC	CZ-2C	July 29, 2011	SSO	98.1°
TC-2	TSLC	CZ-2C	July 25, 2004	HEO	88.47°
NX-1	XSLC	CZ-2C	April 18, 2004	SSO	97.5°
ZP-1B	JSLC	CZ-2D	September 22, 2010	SSO	98.0°
ZP-1C	JSLC	CZ-2D	September 22, 2010	SSO	97.9°
TX-1	TSLC	CZ-4B	November 09, 2011	LEO	97.4°
SY-3	JSLC	CZ-2D	November 05, 2008	LEO	98.5°
SY-4	JSLC	CZ-2D	November 20, 2011	LEO	98.5 °

The Future of China' Satellite Programme

It can be seen that China has been expanding its capabilities in all areas of space applications technology through its satellite programme. In the field of remote sensing, China has stopped depending on imagery recovered many days after observation to near real time imagery transmitted directly from space. China has increased its digital imagery resolution to greater than 2.36 m, has developed 3D imaging ability and has apparently acquired SAR capability which would enable satellites to have day and night coverage and also the ability to see through obstacles like clouds, smoke and fog, and even underwater or underground. In the field of communication, China has acquired semi-global coverage largely on its own. China has indigenously developed its own navigation system which is set to achieve global coverage within a decade, thus, realising complete self-reliance in navigation. The regularity of testing new satellite technologies has increased recently, along with China's experiments with small satellites, enabling it to launch satellites cheaper and with more frequency, further expanding its satellite fleet.

China very well has the realisation that there still exists a large gap between itself and the advanced countries in areas like space science, technology and applications even after completing 40 years of space faring. Also, China's contributions in these areas to its own development as well as to the rest of humanity are disproportionate with its status as a nation with the largest population, and a growing economy on its way to become the largest in the world.[15] Therefore, China has come up with a development strategy and roadmap for space science, applications and technology to 2050, as proposed by the Chinese Academy of Sciences in 2009.

A remarkable amount of contribution to space science is one of the goals explicitly highlighted in the road map. This could mean an ever greater number of scientific satellite launches being conducted in the coming years with missions related to the study of space environment. China lays stress on exploring the unsolved as well as fundamental realms of space science which would be instrumental in creating its own mark in this field. Another likely trend for the future, as could be assessed from the specified goals, is the enhancement of earth observation satellite capabilities to provide adequate data for developing a robust earth observation infrastructure capable of modelling and forecasting environmental changes and resource exploration. To realise the aim of global navigational capability by 2020 through the Beidou project, 25 more satellites needs to be put into the orbit in the next 9 years (almost three satellites per year on average). Considering the fact that during initial period of the second phase for the last 4 years, China has put 10 such satellites in orbit (more than two satellites per year on average), it appears that China could well be on track to achieving its goal. Along with these, the advancement of key technologies related to providing strong technical support to space science as well as applications is also one of the stated goals. This involves developing ultra-high resolution imaging capability, ultra high precision standards, laser communication technology and light satellites and payloads.[16] This obviously point towards the continuation of the miniaturisation trend, but in an accelerated manner which has already started through the development of small satellites like the Tsinghua, Chuang Xin and the Na Xing satellite series.

Supplementing these plans are critical infrastructure developments like the new launch site, which is currently being built at Wenchang in Hainan Island,

and will be operational by 2013.[17] The uniqueness of this launch site will be its proximity to the equator as well as to the eastern sea. The maritime proximity to the east would facilitate launches to orbits having a wide range of inclinations. The equatorial proximity would make launches cheaper due to fuel savings and also facilitate the launch of heavier satellites with more equipments as well as more fuel, especially to the GTO. This would mean that multi-purpose payloads can be launched together and also satellites with longer in-orbit life can be launched as more fuel can be accommodated.

Thus, there are plenty of indicators which predict that the future of China's satellite programme will be characterised by advances in cutting-edge technology as well as high launch rate. In sharp contrast to the earlier China during the formative years of the space programme, today's China has an abundance of technological, material and financial resources as well as skilled manpower. This, along with a highly determined and organised technocracy in command provides a highly facilitating environment for the achievement of the stated strategic goals. One decisive factor which could impede the growth of China's ambitious satellite programme would be the economic trajectory. A severe economic downturn in the future could lead to a space budget crunch, precariously slowing down the programme. However, this possibility can be considered very remote since China has demonstrated its capacity to overcome two such instances in the last two decades.

One major challenge that China will inevitably face in the near future will be the replacement of existing satellites. It can be observed from the launch data that most of the satellites that exist currently in orbit are newly developed and launched towards the latter half of the last decade. This could mean that around and post 2020, a relatively high demand in the need for replacement would arise. This would also coincide with satellite projects like the final launches of the navigational constellation and scientific missions, and projects like the manned lunar programme, Mars and Venus probes, as well as regular supply launches to its space station, expected to be completed by 2020. The future of China's satellite programme would then be very much dependent on how well it would be able to increase the capacity of its satellite fleet within the existing constraints.

The Human Spaceflight Programme

Similar to what happened in the satellite programme, China initiated its manned spaceflight programme after the breakthrough by the Soviet Union. The first human spaceflight in 1965 by Yuri Gagarin led to China commencing 'Project 714', which was intended to develop manned spaceflight capability.[18] It aimed to send humans to space by 1973 through a spacecraft called Shuguang-1 (Dawn in Chinese).[19] The project was the brainchild of Dr. Qian Xuesen as with the case of the satellite programme. He established the Spaceflight Medical Research Centre for this purpose in 1968.[20] Just as the satellite programme came to a halt due to the impact of the Great Leap Forward, Project 714 came to a halt in 1972. This time, it was the Cultural Revolution politics, which interfered with the growth of China's space programme.[21] However, the programme resumed indirectly through the Fanhui Shi Weixing recoverable remote sensing satellite series initiated in 1974. Through this series, China mastered the recovery technology, which is crucial for retrieving any future manned spacecraft. China had to wait until the 1990s to formally re-establish its manned space programme.

The Shenzhou and Human Spaceflight

On September 21, 1992, the Chinese government restarted the manned space programme under 'Project 921'. Its objective was the development of manned spaceflight capabilities and its further advancement. This was planned to be done in three stages. The first sage involved sending humans to space; the second stage involved the establishment of a space station, and the third stage involved the development of reusable launch vehicles. These objectives were to be accomplished within three decades. The programme planned launching the first unmanned test spacecraft by 1998, manned spaceflight by 2002, and a space lab by 2007, leading to the eventual establishment of the space station. Since China was lacking the technological knowhow for implementing the programme, it had to seek for assistance from Russia which had a rich expertise in manned spaceflight. A deal was signed between the two nations in 1995 for the technology transfer of Russia's Soyuz spacecraft. It included training, provision of Soyuz capsules, life support systems, docking systems, and space suits. Two Taikonauts (Chinese astronauts or Yuhangyuans) were trained in Russia's Gagarin Cosmonaut Training Centre in Star City, Moscow from 1996. They came back to China and, in turn, trained the other taikonauts. Simultaneously, China designed its own version of the Soyuz spacecraft called the Shenzhou (Divine Vessel) and also the CZ-2F rocket for the purpose of launching manned missions.[22] The programme itself came to be known as the Shenzhou Programme.

The Shenzhou spacecraft weighs around 8 tonnes and has a three-module design similar to the Apollo (US spacecraft) and Soyuz. It consists of the Service, Recovery and Orbital modules. The Service module powers the spacecraft, being fitted with solar panels. The Recovery module is the main control module and is the only module that is retrieved, in order to carry the Taikonauts back to earth safely. The Orbital module is the living as well as working module of the crew and remains in space after detachment of the other two modules.[23]

Fig. 4.2: Shenzhou Spacecraft

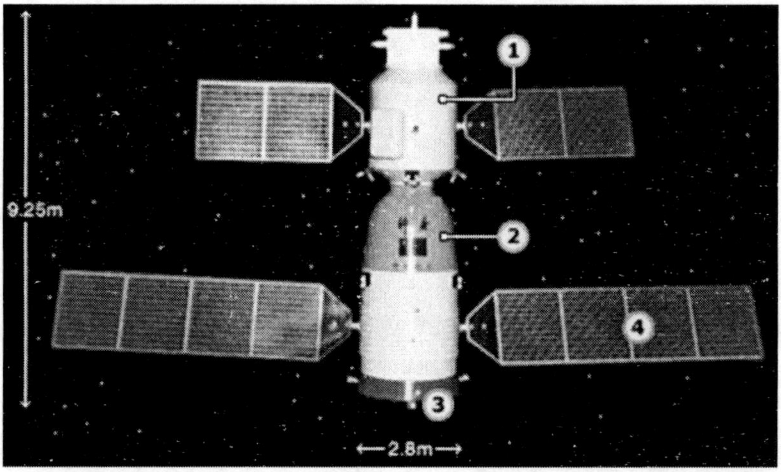

1. Orbital Module
2. Recovery Module
3. Service Module
4. Solar Panel

Source: BBC (http://www.bbc.co.uk)

There have been allegations of the Shenzhou's striking similarity to the Soyuz. It is alleged that an off course unmanned Soyuz might have crash-landed in China, which could have been reverse-engineered. Some experts have countered this view, arguing that the borrowing was only to a limited extent. The fact remains that the Chinese had attempted unsuccessfully to purchase a full Soyuz craft from the Russians, and therefore, had to settle with only the stripped down capsules. Certainly, the Shenzhou has been inspired by the Soyuz as the basic template is found to be the same, both having the fundamental three-module configuration. However, the differences come in the details. The Shenzhou is larger and heavier, and has been assessed to be technologically superior to the Soyuz. The Propulsion module has 4 main engines compared to the Soyuz which has only two – one main and a back-up. The Shenzhou also has additional features like a second set of solar panels and an independent flight control system in the orbital module.[24]

In the initial development stage of the programme, there were certain difficulties, especially with the launch escape system. Also, by the time the rocket was ready for launch, the spacecraft was not. Therefore, the first Shenzhou spacecraft, the Shenzhou-1 was essentially a test craft without any full-fledged instrumentation, except for the most crucial guidance and recovery systems.[25] The first unmanned flight test was carried out in 1999 through the launch of the Shenzhou-1 on November 20. The flight lasted for 21 hours after which the spacecraft re-entered and was recovered. During the flight, the performance and reliability of the CZ-2F rocket was confirmed. All key aspects like launching, tracking, control, communication, landing and recovery were verified. The life guarantee and the posture control system were also tested during the flight.[26] As the spacecraft was only a rudimentary prototype, it was not possible to carry out any experiments in it. The CZ-2F would become the standard workhorse of the Shenzhou missions – both manned and unmanned with the standard launch centre fixed at Jiuquan. Since the rocket has been dedicated for the Shenzhou mission, it also came to be known as the Shenjian (Divine Arrow).

The second unmanned mission, carrying the Shenzhou-2 was launched on January 10, 2001. It orbited for a week in space carrying a monkey, a dog and a rabbit to test the life support system. [27] Among other tests, micro-gravity experiments in space life science, space material, space astronomy and space physics were also carried out during its flight in space. The Shenzhou-2 is stated to be the first formal unmanned Shenzhou spacecraft with an improved structure and performance.[28] Although official sources claim smooth re-entry, there has been a certain amount of scepticism attached to the success. This was attributed to the absence of any released photos showing the recovered spacecraft, unlike the succeeding missions.[29] The third unmanned mission, carrying the Shenzhou-3 was launched on March 25, 2002, which also orbited for a week in space. Among others, this mission tested the emergency escape system and also the effects on humans using dummies, human metabolism simulators and medical monitoring equipment.[30] The success of this mission advanced the Shenzhou project a crucial step closer to its primary objective of sending of humans to space. The fourth unmanned mission carrying the Shenzhou-4 was launched on December 30, 2002, which also orbited for a week and returned after completion of tests.[31] In this spacecraft, taikonauts took part in a countdown exercise inside the command module a few hours before liftoff.[32]

Finally, on October 15, 2003, the first manned spacecraft Shenzhou-5 was launched, carrying Lt. Col. Yang Liwei (of the PLA Air Force) into space. It returned successfully after 21 hours and 23 minutes. Valuble data were collected related to the human living environment and safety, along with the performance, reliability and safety of the various spaceflight systems.[33] Thus, with the Shenzou-5, China became the third nation to accomplish manned spaceflight after Russia and the US. This was perhaps the most significant moment in China's space faring history, after its first satellite launch. According to Zhang Qingwei, the Deputy Director of the Project 921, China has achieved through this mission breakthroughs in 13 key technological areas including re-entry lift control of the manned spacecraft, emergency rescue, soft landing, malfunction diagnosis, module separation and heat prevention.[34] It is estimated that for the manned space programme, China spent almost US$ 2.1 billion from its inception until the first successful manned spaceflight.[35]

The next manned spacecraft, the Shenzhou-6 was launched on October 12, 2005 with two taikonauts on board – Fei Junlong and Nie Haisheng. The main objective of the mission was to master 'multi-person multi-day' spaceflight operations. The taikonauts spent 5 days in orbit, after which they returned safely.[36] The third manned spacecraft, the Shenzhou-7 was launched on September 25, 2008, with three taikonauts – Zhai Zhigang, Liu Boming and Jing Haipeng. During this mission, the main objective was to carry out extra-vehicular activity (EVA) by taikonauts for the first time. After spending 68 hours in space, it returned completing the milestone achievement.[37] The EVAs included a spacewalk, manual retrieval of test samples attached to the spacecraft, verification of the working of the Tianlian Data Relay Satellite, and the release of a small imaging satellite from the spacecraft for the first time, which flew in formation with the craft. This satellite provided valuable data and experience for future docking operations through simulated manoeuvres with the orbital module.[38] The imported Russian as well as the Chinese Feitian ('Fly in space' in Chinese) EVA spacesuits as well as the airlock technology were also tested during the mission.[39] China is the 3rd country in the world to conduct EVA in space as well as possess the associated capabilities. It signalled the capability achieved by China's space programme for conducting manual maintenance activities in space. This is a capability which is vital for maintaining the planned space lab or space station in orbit in the future.

The Tiangong and the Space Station

The next step in the three stage manned space programme was the initiation of the manned space station project. It consists of two phases – the establishment of a space lab by 2016 and a space station by 2020. The developmental work for this stage started in February 1999 as China became confident on launching its first unmanned spacecraft.[40] The space lab would be assembled of three Tiangong (Heavenly palace in Chinese) space lab modules. Taikonauts will be sent to this space lab to conduct experiments as well as to accumulate experience and capability in managing and working in the future space station.[41]

Fig. 4.3: Tiangong-1

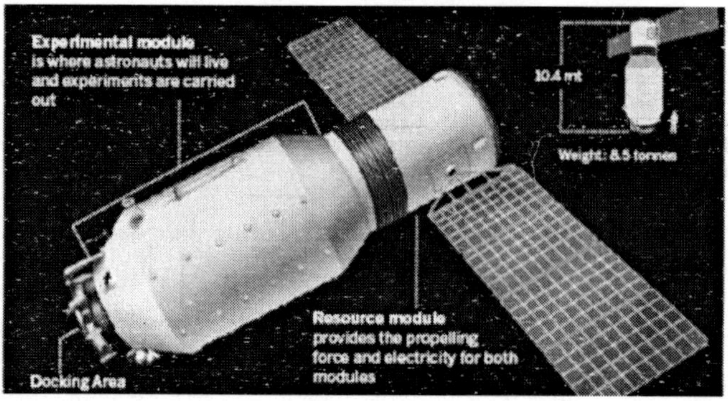

Source: China Daily (http://www.chinadaily.com.cn)

The Tiangong-1, the first space lab module, was developed as an elementary prototype space station and a passive target to master the rendezvous, docking as well as other operations and systems. They include life and work support as well as safety facilities for humans, manned and unmanned experiments, and the overall systems maintenance which are required to establish a full-fledged space station. The Tiangong-1 is China's first spacecraft capable of long term flight and human occupancy (with a three crew member capacity). It weighs around 8.5 tonnes (slightly larger and heavier than Shenzhou spacecraft) and is composed of two modules – the experimental and the resource modules. The experimental module is used for the testing of the rendezvous and docking procedure, and can be used by taikonauts to live and work. There are two sleeping sections with an adjustable lighting system, exercise equipment, entertainment systems, and visual communications equipment in the module. The resource module is used for powering the spacecraft and is hence provided with solar panels.[42] Three Shenzhou spacecrafts (Shenzhou-8, 9 and 10) were planned to dock with the Tiangong-1 in two years.[43] The Tiangong-1 was launched on September 29, 2011 and was followed by the launch of the Shenzhou-8 on 1 November 2011 to test vital docking exercises. After the initial docking, the assembled pair orbited the Earth for 12 days, after which they separated and carried out a second successful docking.[44] The Shenzhou-8 returned after two weeks after accomplishing its crucial objectives. The Tiangong-1 meanwhile, upgraded its orbit waiting for the subsequent dockings with Shenzhou-9 and 10. China's State Intellectual Property Office (SIPO) conferred 15 patent certificates to the SAST, developer of the docking mechanism for China's first space docking mission. China had been working since 1994 on this docking technology.[45]

The two prospective missions to dock with the Tiangong-1 are supposed to be launched in 2012, and one of them would be manned. There are indications that this time, female taikonauts would also be sent. There have been reports of two female taikonauts being trained for these missions.[46] The setting up of the space lab would facilitate in building the space station which China aims to complete by the end of this decade. The Tiangong-2 and Tiangong-3 would be launched by 2013 and 2015 respectively, leading to the establishment of the space lab by 2016.

The proposed space station consists of a core cabin module and two lab modules, all of which would be launched separately in the future. It will weigh about 60 tonnes, much smaller than the 450 tonne International Space Station (ISS). It will act as a large space lab where a wide variety of space experiments would be conducted. It could also be used for replenishment or even refuelling for long missions, including manned planetary explorations. It is supposed to remain active in orbit for a decade. For delivering supplies for replenishment, China will develop an unmanned cargo spacecraft which could weigh about 30 tonnes. It would be composed of two modules – a cargo module for carrying the supplies and a propulsion module for powering the spacecraft. The cabin module for the final space station would be launched in 2020, and the lab modules are planned to be launched in 2021 and 2022. Thus, the space station is supposed become a reality by 2022. The future Chinese space station will be the third of such a kind to be established after the now defunct Mir of erstwhile Soviet Union and the currently operational ISS of the US. Also, it would be the only existing space station as the ISS is set to retire coincidentally by 2022.[47]

Fig. 4.4: The Future Chinese Space Station

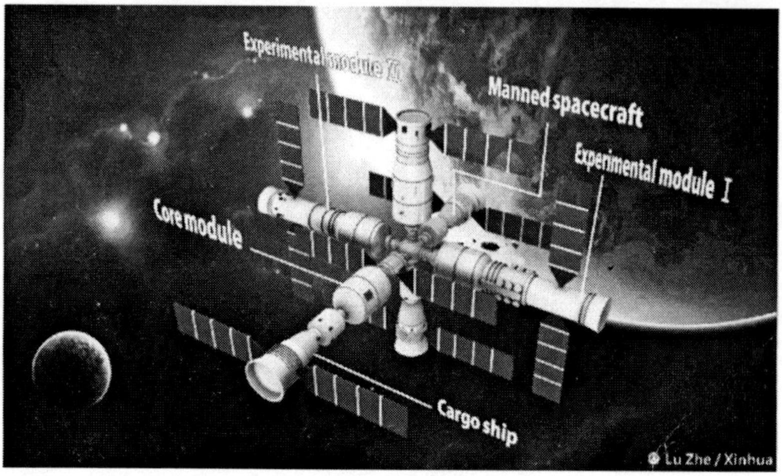

Source: Xinhua News Agency (http://news.xinhuanet.com)

Up to now, China conducted nine launches in its two decade of human spaceflight programme, including one Tiangong and 8 Shenzhou (of which 5 were unmanned and 3 were manned) spacecrafts. The most significant aspect of these launches is the absence of any failed mission. Moreover, China has been largely successful in meeting its objectives as of now in line with the 1992 roadmap. However, these feats come a long time after the Soviet Union and the US have accomplished them. China's maiden human voyage to space, the Shenzhou-5 (2003) was four decades after that of the two established space powers (1961). Similarly, China's first EVA (2008) comes almost four decades after that of the USSR and the US (1965). Even, China's first long term base in space, the Tiangong-1 (2011) comes four decades after the USSR (Salyut-1, 1971) and USA (Skylab, 1973) established their stations. Thus, China can be found to be lagging behind the US and Russia by roughly 40 years in manned spaceflight. Nevertheless, the pace at which China's capabilities are growing in this realm is nothing short of being noteworthy, if not phenomenal for a developing country with a rising power status.

Space Exploration Programme

After achieving the capability to send satellites into space, and decades later followed by manned spaceflight, the next major objective for China was space exploration. The traditional space powers have followed the same path, starting with the Moon, then Mars, asteroids and even beyond. The same was the case with China, with the Moon being the initial stepping stone towards the objective of deep space exploration.

The Chang'e Lunar Exploration Programme

Exploring the Moon becomes important for a rising space power like China as it provides several unique opportunities. Apart from the conditions of vacuum and low gravity which could help in the production of substances with a high degree of purity not possible on earth, it also provides valuable minerals and energy resources. The Helium-3 isotope is by far the most prominent among them. This is because it could be used as a fuel for Nuclear Fusion, considered to be a promising panacea for energy security without pollution risks in the post-Fukushima era. Helium-3, which is scarce on earth, is abundant on the Moon with approximate reserves ranging from 1-5 million tonnes.[48] It is estimated that 25 tonnes of the radioactive isotope would be enough to power a country like the US for one full year.[49] The Moon could also be used as a future base for further deep space exploration activities due to the low gravity conditions facilitating easy launches.

The Chang'e lunar exploration programme is the most prominent part of China's space science programme. It was named after a Chinese Goddess who flew from the earth to the Moon. The Chang'e lunar exploration programme is only the first step of China's space exploration programme. It got evolved as the next significant leap after the Shenzhou programme with a three stage plan. The first stage involves lunar orbiting for surveying and mapping of lunar surface. The second stage is intended to carry out an unmanned lunar landing and surface probing involving a robotic rover. The third stage involves unmanned landing, collecting and returning of lunar surface samples using a second rover. All of this would be a precursor to an eventual manned landing on the Moon.[50] This programme was proposed in 1991. By 2004, the first phase was initiated.[51]

As a part of the first stage, a probe called Chang'e-1 was planned to be sent to the lunar orbit. It had four scientific objectives, which included obtaining 3D imagery of the lunar surface, detecting the contents and distribution of useful chemical elements on the lunar surface, probing the properties of lunar regolith, and exploring the space environment between the earth and the Moon.[52] It also had four technological objectives, which included developing and launching China's first lunar orbiter, testing the lunar orbiting technologies, starting scientific exploration of the Moon, developing the basic engineering system for lunar exploration and accumulating experience for subsequent lunar explorations.[53] The Chang'e-1 was launched on October 24, 2007 on-board the CZ-3A rocket from Xichang, and it entered the lunar orbit 14 days later. With this, China became the 4th country to conduct lunar orbiting after US, Russia and Japan. At an altitude of 200 km above the lunar surface, the probe conducted 3D mapping using stereo cams and X-ray spectrometers. The main objective of this probe was to map potential lunar resources.[54] It sent back both 2D and 3D images of the lunar surface and finally ended its mission by crashing onto the surface of the Moon after 16 months on March 2009.[55]

This was followed on October 01, 2010 by the launch of a second probe, the Chang'e 2 on a CZ-3C rocket from Xichang.[56] This orbiter was launched for continuing the objectives of the previous missions, but in much greater detail. In addition to this, the probe was also meant to identify a suitable landing area for the second stage of the Chang'e mission.[57] The Chang'e-2 weighed 2.48 tonnes and had a life of about 6 months. Unlike its predecessor, it orbited closer to the lunar surface at an elevation of 100 km, getting a clearer view of the surface. Most importantly, it took the images of the Sinus Iridium (Bay of Rainbows) and other four potential landing spots for the second phase of the Chang'e programme.[58] This marked the success of the Chang'e-2 mission.

The second stage of the Chang'e programme which involves a robotic rover is expected to be launched in 2013.[59] This rover would detect, collect and analyse lunar surface samples. The third stage for collection of lunar samples will be launched by 2017.[60] According to the current design of a sample collector, 2 kg of lunar samples can be brought back from the Moon.[61]

The Chang'e missions were a real test of China's TT&C capabilities. China successfully controlled the probes, which were at a distance of 4,00,000 km away from the earth, ten times more distant than any of its farthest satellites.[62] The successes gained will be utilised by China to further advance its space programme. Dr. Joan Johnson Freese, a professor at the US Naval war College remarked that the Shenzhou and the Chang'e missions 'seem clearly intended to eventually be linked toward a human spaceflight mission to the Moon'.[63] This momentous culmination of both the projects is supposed to get materialised around 2025.[64] With the capability to send humans to the Moon, China could then move forward with lunar mining to extract the valuable lunar resources. Through the 2011 White Paper on its space activities, China has stated that it has studied the lunar morphology, structure, surface matter composition, microwave properties, and near-Moon space environment through its previous lunar missions. It has also declared its plans to push forward its exploration of planets, asteroids and the sun of the solar system.[65]

The Exploration of Mars

With its lunar exploration programme underway, China initiated its next ambitious initiative – a Mars exploration programme. However, unlike the lunar mission, China was unable to perform the mission independently. Compared to the eight to nine day journey to the Moon, the journey to Mars would take about nine to ten months. Because China has not yet developed the capability for such long distance spaceflight, it had to, therefore, depend upon Russia to accomplish the task. On March 26, 2007, both the CNSA and the Russian Space Agency signed a co-operative agreement on the joint exploration of Mars.[66] The Yinghuo-1 (Firefly in Chinese) orbiter was developed for this purpose. Its mission involved the exploration of the external Martian environment and the solar wind-planet interaction.[67] The Yinhghuo-1 weighs only about 115 kg and would orbit Mars at an 800 x 80,000 km orbit. It would also probe certain regions of the Martian ionosphere which were unexplored by earlier Mars missions.[68] This probe was clubbed along with Russia's first planetary exploration mission. The Russian mission consisted of a robotic spacecraft called Phobos-Grunt, which was supposed to land in Phobos (a satellite of Mars), from which it had to carry back soil samples.[69] The Yinghuo-1 would be piggybacked on this spacecraft and launched into the Martian orbit where it will carry out its mission during its period of life of about a year.[70] Both the probes were also supposed to carry out co-ordinated measurements on the Martian environment.[71] The Phobos-Grunt/ Yinghuo-1 probes were launched on November 08, 2011 at 2016 UT on a Zenit 2SB41.1 rocket from the Baikonur Cosmodrome in Kazakhstan. However, a firing failure resulted in the failure of the mission with the duo lingering in the Earth orbit.[72]

This failure has become an exception to China's otherwise successful maiden space attempts.[73] The next mission is apparently possible only by 2016. The Chinese will then be unable to make it to Mars before the US sends a similar probe by 2013. According to Wu Ji, Director-General of the National Space Science Centre under the Chinese Academy of Sciences, the failure has led to a loss of a vital opportunity to surpass the US in conducting breakthrough research on the Martian atmosphere, an unexplored realm.[74] However, once success is achieved, China is also planning to send humans to Mars. This is evident from the participation of the Taikonaut Wang Ye in the Mars-500 project, which concluded in January 2012. This project was conducted by the Russian Academy of Sciences in co-operation with the European Space Agency and the Astronaut Centre of China (ACC), in which he was part of a six-member crew who underwent a 520-day long simulation in long distance spaceflight to and from Mars as well as surface landing.[75] Meanwhile, China has set its ambitions even further with its first Venus probe planned for 2015.[76] However, the whole of China's planetary exploration depends upon the decisive 2016 re-launch of its Mars probe, whose fate is inextricably linked to Russia's ability to avoid any further failure.

Commercial Space Programme

The commercial space activities of China currently involve satellite export as well as launches. China entered into the commercial space domain in 1986, following the liberalisation and opening up of its economy. China felt increasingly confident with the success it had with the CZ series of rockets, and therefore decided to utilise its launch capabilities to gain commercial benefit from the domestic as well as international launch market. Xichang provided an ideal space launch centre for commercial launches, which was fully operational by then.

Since the US is the leading provider of equipment and services for satellites, its export license policies play a major role in the growth of China's commercial space launches. The changing dynamics in the US policies towards China had led to export licenses being suspended and reinstated at various instances. One of the first such instances was after the Tiananmen Square incident in 1989, when the Sr. Bush Administration of the US suspended and finally lifted sanctions.[77] Then in 1991, sanctions were re-imposed by the same administration against Chinese space organisations accusing them of selling missiles to Pakistan, Iraq and Iran. The launch market picked up considerable momentum only since the mid-1990. Leading upto 2000, China managed to carry out 18 commercial launches at lower prices than the US and the EU. However, a US embargo during the late 1990s over inconsistent transfer of technology combined with the collapse of LEO satellite communication market, led to the stalling of China's commercial space programme for a short while in the initial decade of the 21st century.[78] It started in 1996, when the IntelSat-7A as well as the domestic satellite ChinaSat-7 failed in a row. The IntelSat failure kicked off a chain of events which led to the Sino-US space co-operation reaching its lowest point since the start of the commercial space programme. The company which manufactured the satellite, Space Systems/ Loral reviewed the findings of the Chinese investigations upon the request of insurance companies on the failure and submitted the report to China first rather than to the US. This resulted in allegations from the US on improper transfer of sensitive US technology by these firms to China. Hence, tight export control laws were introduced by the US to restrict the flow of American space technology to China in 1999, strangling the Chinese commercial space programme.[79]

The commercial activities were reinstated later mainly due to orders coming in from the developing countries like Brazil, especially in the wake of the success of the Shenzhou missions. China then started using its space capabilities to develop and launch the first satellites of many countries of the developing world. In 2004, China won the contract for launching Nigeria's first commercial satellite, the NigComSat-1. It was successfully launched in May 2007; however, the satellite failed in orbit prematurely due to solar array anomaly.[80] Therefore, another deal was reached between the two nations to replace the failed satellite by a new one, the NigComSat-1R in March 2009. This was launched successfully on December 20, 2011.[81] The contract with Nigeria turned out to be a breakthrough event, which led to orders coming in from developing countries, where a number of emerging nations have been aspiring to make their presence felt in space and to utilise it for their national development and modernization.. China made an agreement with Venezuela in 2005 to build and launch telecommunication satellites, leading to the successful launch of VeneSat-1 in 2008.[82] This was followed by the launch of Palapa-D1, an Indonesian telecommunications satellite on August 31, 2009, which faced an anomaly in orbit delivery. In October 2008, China signed a contract with Pakistan to develop and launch its first telecommunication satellite PakSat-1R, which was expedited successfully on August 2011.[83] Further deals were struck for future launches after the successful execution of orders from Nigeria, Pakistan and Venezuela. In February 2010, China signed a contract with Laos to develop and launch its first telecommunications satellite, the LaoSat-1.[84] Following this, in December 2010, China signed a contract with Bolivia to develop and launch its first telecommunications satellite, the Tupak Katari.[85] It would be manufactured and launched by China into orbit by 2013. The majority of the cost of these projects were covered by Chinese loans and were given at affordable costs.[86]

Table-4.5: China's Commercial Launch Record

No.	Payload	Customer	Country	Launch Vehicle	Launch Date
1	Micro-gravity Test Instrument	Matra Marconi Space	France/UK	CZ-2C	August 05, 1987
2	Micro-gravity Test Instrument	Infospace	Germany	CZ-2C	August 05, 1988
3	AsiaSat-1	AsiaSat	Hong Kong	CZ-3	August 07, 1990
4	Badr-A	Space and Upper Atmosphere Research Commission (SUPARCO)	Pakistan	CZ-2E	July 16, 1990
5	AusSat-B1	AusSat	Australia	CZ-2E	August 14, 1992
6	Freja	Swedish Space Corporation (SSC)	Sweden	CZ-2C	October 06, 1992
7	Optus-B2*	AusSat	Australia	CZ-2E	December 21, 1992
8	APStar-1	APT Corporation	Hong Kong	CZ-3	July 21, 1994
9	Optus-B3	AusSat	Australia	CZ-2E	August 28, 1994
10	APStar-2*	APT Corporation	Hong Kong	CZ-2E	January 26, 1995
11	AsiaSat-2	AsiaSat	Hong Kong	CZ-2E	November 28, 1995
12	EchoStar-1	EchoStar	USA	CZ-2E	December 28, 1995
13	IntelSat-7A*	IntelSat	International Consortium	CZ-3B	February 15, 1996
14	APStar-1A	APT Corporation	Hong Kong	CZ-3	July 03, 1996
15	ChinaSat-7*	China Direct Broadcast Satellite Company (China DBSAT)	China	CZ-3	August 18, 1996
16	Micro-gravity Test Instrument	Marubeni Corporation	Japan	CZ-2D	October 20, 1996
17	MabuhaySat	Mabuhay Satellite Corporation	The Philippines	CZ-3B	August 20, 1997
18	APStar-2R	APT Corporation	Hong Kong	CZ-3B	October 17, 1997
19	Iridium	Motorola	USA	CZ-2C/SD	December 08, 1997
20	Iridium	Motorola	USA	CZ-2C/SD	March 26, 1998
21	Iridium	Motorola	USA	CZ-2C/SD	May 02, 1998
22	ChinaStar-1	China DBSAT	China	CZ-3B	May 30, 1998
23	SinoSat-1	China DBSAT	China	CZ-3B	July 18, 1998
24	Iridium	Motorola	USA	CZ-2C/SD	August 20, 1998

25	Iridium	Motorola	USA	CZ-2C/ SD	December 19, 1999
26	Iridium	Motorola	USA	CZ-2C/ SD	June 12, 1999
27	CBERS-1	National Institute for Space Research (INPE)	Brazil	CZ-4	October 14, 1999
28	SACI	INPE	Brazil	CZ-4	October 14, 1999
29	CBERS-02	INPE	Brazil	CZ-4	October 21, 2003
30	APStar-6	APT Corporation	Hong Kong	CZ-3B	April 12, 2005
31	NigComSat-1**	National Space Research and Development Agency (NASRDA)	Nigeria	CZ-3B	May 14, 2007
32	ChinaSat-6B	China DBSAT	China	CZ-3B	July 05, 2007
33	CBERS-2B	INPE	Brazil	CZ-3B	September 19, 2007
34	ChinaSat-9	China DBSAT	China	CZ-3B	July 09, 2008
35	VeneSat-1	Ministry of Science and Technology	Venezuela	CZ-3B	October 30, 2008
36	Palapa-D1	Telkom Indonesia	Indonesia	CZ-3B	August 31, 2009
37	PakSat-1R	SUPARCO	Pakistan	CZ-3B	August 12, 2011
39	NigComSat-1R	NASRDA	Nigeria	CZ-3B	December 20, 2011

* Launch failures ** Satellite failure

Fig. 4.5: China's Commercial Launch Statistics

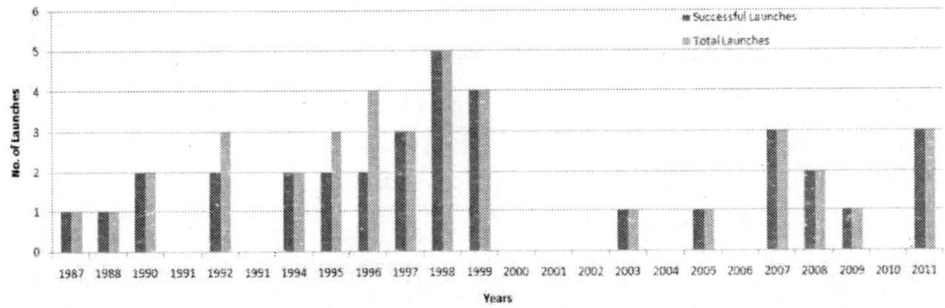

Source: China Great Wall Industry Corporation (http://www.cgwic.com)

China has undertaken 39 commercial launches from 1987, out of which 4 were failures, and therefore, has a success rate touching 90 per cent. However, this quantitatively high success rate has little relevance to the trajectory of the programme, as the few failures had visibly more significant, yet adverse impact. Among the launches, 30 were launches for international customers, and the remaining 9 were for domestic customers. A total of 15 international customers and 3 domestic customers were served by the Chinese commercial space programme since its inception. The foreign customers include private and state owned corporations and national space agencies from 13 nations, an almost balanced mix of 7 developed and 6 developing countries. The domestic customers included the state owned corporations in the mainland as well as the private corporations in Hong Kong. Up to 1999, most of the customers were from the developed world. However, since 1999, the launch orders have seen a shift in trend, as more and more orders started coming from the developing world also. Almost two-thirds of the international launches were for the customers from developed nations in this recent period. Considering the entire programme history, the maximum number of foreign orders came from the US with 7 launches, followed by Brazil with 4 launches and Australia with 3 launches.

China's outstanding track record of successful launches and its low cost has great potential in creating its own space in the global commercial launch market. Nevertheless, the restrictions imposed by the US have gravely impeded the momentum in which the programme was growing in the 1990s. This in turn had led China to search for new markets where it could export its satellites, built without any content of US technology. Nigeria, Pakistan, Venezuela, and currently Bolivia and Laos have emerged as not only new markets but could also prove as gateways to the emerging markets of Africa and Latin America. The Indonesian satellite, Palapa-D1 made by the European company Thales Alenia Space, was a major breakthrough in this regard as it did not use any technological content from the US, even though its 2009 faced an anomaly in orbital delivery.[87] Currently, China's share in the global commercial launch market which is dominated by the US, Russia and Europe, remains very low and has not picked up significantly.[88] By 2015, China aims to capture 10 per cent of the international commercial satellite market, and 15 per cent of the world commercial space launch service market. China is also expected to widen its commercial space programme by initiating services in sectors including satellite management, capital investment and aerospace information software, among others.[89] With the commercial communications satellite launch costs almost 40 per cent less than existing programmes, China is emerging as a low cost alternative for space launches.[90] In addition, China's increasing engagement with the developing world is bound to create new opportunities for its commercial space realm. This is especially so as confidence is building up in its space industry marked by booming launch rates, high levels of success, adherence to time limits as well as expanding domain and capabilities.

Notes

1. Information regarding satellites are compiled from the following sources along with some own assessments: Satellite details are obtained from the NASA National Space Science Data Centre (NSSDC) website http://nssdc.gsfc.nasa.gov/nmc/spacecraftSearch.do; activity status of satellites in orbit are obtained from Celestrak website http://celestrak.com/; and satellite launch details are obtained from the news archives of China Aerospace Science and Technology Corporation (CASC) website http://www.spacechina.com/english/news.shtml, accessed on July 13, 2011.
2. White paper on China's Space Activities released in 2006, see http://www.china.org.cn/english/features/book/183715.htm, accessed on June 25, 2011.
3. Optical imaging is a method of remote sensing which uses visible light to obtain images. Infra red imaging is a method of remote sensing that obtains images of radiation in the infra-red region of the electromagnetic spectrum (radiated heat) from the observed objects, the temperature variations being represented by different colours in the image. Multi-spectral imaging is a method of remote sensing that obtains optical representations in two or more ranges of frequencies all across the electromagnetic spectrum and thus capable of sensing more detail. See the United States Geological Survey (USGS) website, http://www.usgs.gov/science/science.php?term=981, accessed on September 11, 2011.
4. B. Bizzari, "Dossier on the Space-based Component of the Global Observing System (GOS-2011)", see ftp://ftp.wmo.int/Documents/PublicWeb/sat/DossierGOS/, accessed on July 16, 2011.
5. "Ziyuan 2", see http://www.sinodefence.com/space/satellite/ziyuan2.asp, accessed on July 16, 2011.
6. "Yaogan", see http://www.sinodefence.com/space/military/yaogan.asp, accessed on July 13, 2011.
7. China Academy of Space Technology, "Satellite Equipments", see http://www.cast.cn/CastEn/Special.asp?SpecialID=17, accessed on July 13, 2011.
8. n. 28, p. 82.
9. n. 33.
10. Satellite details obtained from see China Satellite Communications Co. Ltd. website see http://www.chinasatcom.com/en/News_Info.aspx?m=20110329113845577061&n=20110329133705937193, accessed on July 17, 2011.
11. n. 28, pp. 77- 78; "Shentong (ChinaSat 20)", see http://www.sinodefence.com/space/military/st.asp; and "Fenghuo", http://www.sinodefence.com/space/military/fenghuo.asp, accessed on July 17, 2011.
12. n. 42.
13. n. 33.

14. Ibid.
15. H. Guo and J. Wu, *Space Science and Technology in China: A Roadmap to 2050* (Beijing: Science Press, 2010), p. 43.
16. Ibid.
17. R. Rao, "China's Space Programme", see http://www.ipcs.org/article/china/chinas-space-programme-2977.html, accessed on April 22, 2011.
18. F. Cunningham, "The Stellar Status Symbol: True Motives for China's Manned Space Program", China *Security*, vol. 5, no. 3, 2009, p. 80, see http://www.chinasecurity.us/pdfs/FionaCunningham.pdf, accessed on December 25, 2011.
19. J.A. Lewis, "Surmounting the Peak: China's Space Program", November 2005, p. 1, see http://csis.org/files/media/csis/pubs/051116_china_space_program.pdf, accessed on December 25, 2011.
20. Fultron Corporation, "China and the Second Space Age", October 15, 2003, p. 5, see http://www.futron.com/upload/wysiwyg/Resources/Whitepapers/China_n_%20Second_Space_Age_1003.pdf, accessed on December 27, 2011.
21. n. 50.
22. n. 52, p. 6.
23. n. 19, p. 2.
24. J. Oberg, "China's Great Leap Upward", *Scientific American Magazine,* October 2003, see http://www.scientificamerican.com/article.cfm?id=chinas-great-leap-upward, accessed on December 28, 2011.
25. n. 6, p. 19.
26. China Manned Space Engineering Office, "Shenzhou-1", see http://en.cmse.gov.cn/list.php?catid=56, accessed on December 26, 2011.
27. n. 56.
28. China Manned Space Engineering Office, "Shenzhou-2", see http://en.cmse.gov.cn/list.php?catid=57, accessed on December 26, 2011.
29. n. 6, p. 20.
30. China Manned Space Engineering Office, "Shenzhou-3", see http://en.cmse.gov.cn/list.php?catid=58, accessed on December 26, 2011.
31. China Manned Space Engineering Office, "Shenzhou-4", see http://en.cmse.gov.cn/list.php?catid=59, accessed on December 26, 2011.
32. n. 56.
33. China Manned Space Engineering Office, "Shenzhou-5", see http://en.cmse.gov.cn/list.php?catid=60, accessed on December 26, 2011.
34. J. J. Freese, "China's Space Ambitions", *IFRI Proliferation Papers*, Summer 2007, p. 14, see http://www.ifri.org/downloads/China_Space_Johnson_Freese.pdf, accessed on

December 28, 2011.

35. n. 6, p. 44.

36. China Manned Space Engineering Office, "Shenzhou-6", see http://en.cmse.gov.cn/list.php?catid=61, accessed on December 26, 2011.

37. China Manned Space Engineering Office, "Shenzhou-7", see http://en.cmse.gov.cn/list.php?catid=62, accessed on December 26, 2011.

38. n. 6, p. 193.

39. A. Krolikowski, "China's Civil and Commercial Space Activities and their Implications", p. 13, see http://www.gwu.edu/~spi/assets/docs/11_05_11_krolikowski_testimony.pdf, accessed on December 28, 2011.

40. n. 52, p. 7.

41. n. 71, pp. 7-8.

42. M. Freeman, "China Achieves its Next Milestone in Space Exploration", November 25, 2011, p. 59, see http://www.21stcenturysciencetech.com/Articles_2011/China_Space_Milestone.pdf, accessed on December 30, 2011.

43. China Manned Space Engineering Office, "Tiangong-1", see http://en.cmse.gov.cn/list.php?catid=55, accessed on December 26, 2011.

44. n. 74, p. 57.

45. "China's Space Docking Technology Granted 15 Patent Certificates", *Xinhua News Agency*, November 22, 2011, see http://news.xinhuanet.com/english2010/sci/2011-11/22/c_131263351.htm, accessed on January 02, 2012.

46. n. 74, p. 58.

47. n. 71, pp. 7-14.

48. "Lunar Exploration Close to Daily Life: Experts", *Xinhua News Agency*, October 01, 2010, see http://news.xinhuanet.com/english2010/database/2010-10/01/c_13539256.htm, accessed on January 05, 2011.

49. D. Irvine, "Mining the Moon for a Nuclear Future", see http://articles.cnn.com/2006-12-18/tech/fs.moonmining_1_helium-3-moon-base-nuclear-fusion?_s=PM:TECH, accessed on January 05, 2012.

50. n. 15, p. 3.

51. China National Space Administration, "China's Lunar Exploration Activities: Milestones of the Program", see http://www.cnsa.gov.cn/n615709/n772514/n772543/index.html, accessed on January 03, 2012.

52. China Aerospace Science and Technology Corporation, "Chang'e-1", see http://www.spacechina.com/n16421/n17215/n17269/n19037/c125365/content.html, accessed on January 04, 2012.

53. n. 56.

54. J. Logan, "China's Space Program: Options for US-China Cooperation", *CRS Report for Congress*, September 29, 2008, p. 5, see http://www.fas.org/sgp/crs/row/RS22777.pdf, accessed on February 10, 2011.
55. n. 84.
56. "China's 2nd Lunar Probe Chang'e-2 Blasts Off", *Xinhua News Agency*, October 01, 2010, see http://news.xinhuanet.com/english2010/sci/2010-10/01/c_13539035.htm, accessed on January 07, 2012.
57. China Aerospace Science and Technology Corporation, "Chang'e-2", see http://www.spacechina.com/n16421/n17215/n17269/n19037/c125359/content.html, accessed on January 05, 2012.
58. "Chang'e-2 Completes Mission, Chang'e-3 to be Launched in 2013", *Xinhua News Agency,* April 02, 2011, see http://news.xinhuanet.com/english2010/video/2011-04/02/c_13810410.htm, accessed on January 06, 2012.
59. C. Moskowitz , "China's Lofty Goals: Space Station, Moon and Mars exploration", December 06, 2010, see http://www.space.com/10431-china-lofty-goals-space-station-moon-mars-exploration.html, accessed on January 05, 2012.
60. n. 86.
61. "China Considering Manned Lunar Landing in 2025-2030", *Xinhua News Agency*, May 24, 2009, see http://news.xinhuanet.com/english/2009-05/24/content_11425131.htm, accessed on January 07, 2012.
62. "Factbox: China's Pride in Lunar Probe", *Xinhua News Agency*, December 12, 2007, see http://news.xinhuanet.com/english/2007-12/12/content_7235576.htm, accessed on January 08, 2012.
63. "Foreign Scholars, Media Hail China's Launch of 2nd Lunar Probe", *Xinhua News Agency*, October 02, 2010, see http://news.xinhuanet.com/english2010/sci/2010-10/02/c_13540353.htm, accessed on January 08, 2012.
64. "Moon Landing Gets Timetable", *People's Daily*, September 20, 2010, see http://english.peopledaily.com.cn/90001/90776/90881/7145453.html, accessed on January 09, 2012.
65. Chinese Central Government, "China's Space Activities in 2011", see http://www.gov.cn/english/official/2011-12/29/content_2033200.htm, accessed on January 05, 2012.
66. "China and Russia Join Hands to Explore Mars", *People's Daily*, May 30, 2007, see http://english.peopledaily.com.cn/200705/30/eng20070530_379330.html, accessed on January 09, 2012.
67. NASA National Space Science Data Centre, "Yinghuo-1", see http://nssdc.gsfc.nasa.gov/nmc/spacecraftDisplay.do?id=YINGHUO-1, accessed on January 10, 2012.
68. Z. Hua, "YingHuo-1: Martian Space Environment Exploration Orbiter", *Chinese Journal of Space Science*, vol. 28, no. 5, 2008, p. 395, see http://www.cjss.ac.cn/qikan/manage/

wenzhang/2008-05-06.pdf, accessed on January 10, 2012.

69. "Russia Launches Probe to Mars Moon", *RIANovosti*, November 09, 2011, see http://en.rian.ru/science/20111109/168527324.html, accessed on January 10, 2012.
70. n. 98.
71. n. 100, p. 396
72. n. 99.
73. "Moon Landing Gets Timetable", *People's Daily*, September 20, 2010, see http://english.peopledaily.com.cn/90001/90776/90881/7145453.html, accessed on January 05, 2012.
74. "Failure of Mission hits Mars research", *Xinhua News Agency*, January 20, 2012, see http://news.xinhuanet.com/english/sci/2012-01/20/c_131370239_2.htm, accessed on January 21, 2012.
75. W. Ru, "Lost in Simulated Space", *China Daily*, January 18, 2012, see http://www.chinadaily.com.cn/cndy/2012-01/18/content_14465115.htm, accessed on January 21, 2012.
76. n. 105.
77. n. 16, p. 4.
78. n. 52, p. 6.
79. G. Xiaobing, "Blockade on China or the United States? US Regulatory Policies on Space Technology Exports to China", see http://www.chinasecurity.us/index.php?option=com_content&view=article&id=249&Itemid=8, accessed on January 22, 2012.
80. China Great Wall Industry Corporation, "NigComSat-1 Program", see http://www.cgwic.com/In-OrbitDelivery/CommunicationsSatellite/Program/NigComSat-1.html, accessed on January 22, 2012.
81. China Great Wall Industry Corporation, "NigComSat-1R Program", see http://www.cgwic.com/In-OrbitDelivery/CommunicationsSatellite/Program/NigComSat-1R.html, accessed on January 23, 2012.
82. China Great Wall Industry Corporation, "VeneSat-1 Program", see http://www.cgwic.com/In-OrbitDelivery/CommunicationsSatellite/Program/VeneSat-1.html, accessed on January 23, 2012.
83. China Great Wall Industry Corporation, "PakSat-1R Program", see http://www.cgwic.com/In-OrbitDelivery/CommunicationsSatellite/Program/PakSat-1R.html, accessed on January 23, 2012.
84. China Great Wall Industry Corporation, "LaoSat-1 Program", see http://www.cgwic.com/In-OrbitDelivery/CommunicationsSatellite/Program/Laos.html, accessed on January 23, 2012.
85. China Great Wall Industry Corporation, "Tupak Katari Program", see http://www.cgwic.com/In-OrbitDelivery/CommunicationsSatellite/Program/Bolivia.html, accessed on

January 23, 2012.

86. J. C. Moltz, "China's Space Technology: International Dynamics and Implications for the United States", see http://www.uscc.gov/hearings/2011hearings/written_testimonies/11_05_11_wrt/11_05_11_moltz_testimony.pdf, accessed on January 23, 2012.
87. R. Cliff, C.J.R. Ohlandt and D. Yang, "Ready for Takeoff: China's Advancing Aerospace Industry", *RAND Corporation Monograph*, see http://www.rand.org/content/dam/rand/pubs/monographs/2011/RAND_MG1100.pdf, accessed on 24 January 2012.
88. J. Fuller, Jr., J. Foust, C. Frappier, D. Kaiser, and D. Vaccaro, "The Commercial Space Industry: A Critical Spacepower Consideration", in C. D. Lutes, P. L. Hays, V. A. Manzo, L. M. Yambrick and M. E. Bunn (eds.),
Toward a Theory of Spacepower (USA: National Defence University, 2011), see http://www.ndu.edu/press/lib/pdf/spacepower/spacepower.pdf, accessed on January 24, 2012.
89. "China to Build World-Class Space Industry in 7 Years", *China Daily*, July 25, 2008, see http://www.chinadaily.com.cn/china/2008-07/25/content_6878471.htm, accessed on January 24, 2012.
90. D. Houpt, "A New Policy Typology to Better Understand the Goals of China's Space Program", *The Space Review*, October 31, 2011, see http://www.thespacereview.com/article/1958/1, accessed on January 25, 2012.

5. China and Space Weaponisation

Militarisation and weaponisation of space are two very important terms which are used in connection with space security, both of which are related but different. Militarisation of space implies the use of space in supporting the ground, naval and air operations conducted by the armed forces. It refers to the development of assets such as early warning, communications, command and control, navigation and monitoring for military purposes. Militarisation of space, therefore, started way back with the placement of the first satellite in outer space. Satellites have been used widely in the force enhancement of military operations like Operation Desert Storm (Iraq, 1991), Operation Allied Force (Kosovo, 1999), Operation Enduring Freedom (Afghanistan, 2002) and Operation Iraqi Freedom (Iraq, 2003). Hence, space militarization has more or less being considered as business as usual. In contrast, weaponisation which involves deployment of weapons in space has not been carried out so far in a full-fledged manner. However, with an increase in space activity and an increase in the militarisation of space, it is highly probable that in future space will itself become a battleground and nations would try to deploy weapons for offence as well as defence in space. There have been arguments that space weaponisation is already underway because some consider the use of space by Ballistic Missile Defence (BMD) systems as capable of destroying not only ballistic missiles, but also space assets. The main issue with such weaponisation of space is that it would hamper the strategic balance and stability existing in the international system and would therefore lead to an arms race.

Preventing space weaponisation has been a regularly discussed and debated topic among the international community. The talks on bringing out an international treaty on the issue have been ongoing in the UN General Assembly (UNGA) since 1981 and the Conference on Disarmament (CD), Geneva since 1985. The UNGA had been adopting the resolutions on 'Prevention of Arms Race in Outer Space' (PAROS) on a regular basis since last thirty one years. Despite achieving widespread approval, there has been no effort to bring in a legally binding agreement on the issue. The negotiations on the same, which have been ongoing in the CD, have also not borne any fruit. This has mostly been due to the adamant stand of the US which has been continuously opposing any such treaty coming into effect in order to protect its strategic interests in space.

The earlier established treaties have only at their best restricted nations from not deploying any weapons of mass destruction in space, and do not guarantee the same for other types of potent weapons. The Partial Test Ban Treaty of 1963 banned Nuclear weapon tests in outer space. The Outer Space Treaty of 1967 banned the deployment of Weapons of Mass Destruction in outer space and discouraged military activity on celestial bodies. However, it does not prohibit their transit as well as deployment of conventional weapons. It also declared liability of states for damage caused by its space objects on another. This was followed in 1972 by the Liability Convention, which established liability mechanisms to compensate for damages caused by space objects of one nation on another. However, the limited space surveillance procedures impede the effective implementation of the treaty. The Launch Registration Convention of 1975 requires national registration of objects launched into space by states and keeping the UN Secretary General informed. It was aimed at promoting transparency, accountability and confidence-building in space. However, the purpose and details of the space missions were not included in its scope. The Environmental Modification Convention of 1976 banned the application of modification techniques on the environment (including outer space) for hostile purposes.

The Moon Agreement of 1979 complemented the Outer Space Treaty by prohibiting all non-peaceful activities on and around the Moon.[1] In addition to these international treaties, there were also UN resolutions like the 47/68 and 1962 (XVIII), which were passed which had relation to space weaponisation. The former was on the 'Principles Relevant to the Use of Nuclear Power Sources in Outer Space', and the latter was on the 'Declaration of Legal Principles Governing the Activities of States in the Exploration on Uses of Outer Space', both of which established a code of conduct in space, but lacked any effectiveness due to their not being legally binding. Apart from the inadequacies within these established treaties, there have been lots of basic flaws in the established international space law. Certain fundamental terms have been kept ambiguous so as to cater to the interest of certain nations, since they can use these loopholes to justify their activities in outer space. The use of the words 'peaceful use' in all these treaties has not been defined legally in international law. The currently existing dominant interpretation of the term is synonymous to non-aggressive applications of space. This clearly gives scope for using space for weaponisation by terming it as a defensive action. Even the term 'Outer Space' is not well defined in legal terms.

There are many interpretations as to where outer space starts. According to the Karman line theory, outer space begins at 100 km from the earth's surface, and is the most prevalent limit accepted by the international space community. Yet another way in which nations have been manipulating such treaties have been to associate it with the UN charter, which confers the right of self-defence on states.[2] This has, therefore, been used in militarising and to some extent, weaponising space. Therefore, there is a need to not only create an anti-space weaponisation regime, but also a well-defined one, which alone can be effective for the cause. A treaty like PAROS gains salience in this context.

China has been emerging as a vocal supporter of a proposed treaty on PAROS since more than a decade. It started in 2000 by bringing out its first working paper in CD against space weaponisation. Along with Russia, China has been working gradually towards the establishment of a regime which could prevent space weaponisation. However, the testing of an ASAT weapon by China in 2007 on one of its defunct weather satellite has raised significant concerns about China's shift in its intent on space weaponisation. It has also raised concerns on an emerging arms race in space among the emerging space faring nations. Nevertheless, China appears to have moved on with its efforts on putting a ban on space weaponisation, a move which requires to be analysed in detail so as to ascertain the consistency between its action and rhetoric.

China acknowledges the fact that weaponisation of space is in no state's interest and therefore supports its ban. But China is at the same time concerned about the US attempts at space weaponisation. There has been a clear move from the US intent in weaponising space, as evident from its policy documents. They are seeking to develop as well as deploy ASAT and space-based weapons so as to defend its space assets, denying adversaries the ability to use their assets, intercepting ballistic missiles and ground targeting from space. Therefore, to understand China's stand on space weaponisation, it is essential to know the US moves on the issue.

The US Factor in China's Strategic Planning in Space

The US has always been opposing international negotiations against space weaponisation, as it had a potential superiority in the development of space weapons and its BMD programme. It wanted to maintain this exclusive edge it had over space, and did not want to give it up. The US doggedly resisted the negotiation of PAROS, at the same time preferring bilateral negotiations with the Soviet Union instead. Further, as signs of an imminent collapse of the Soviet bloc became clear, the US opposed PAROS with the argument that it 'has not identified any practical outer space arms control measures that can be dealt within a multilateral environment'.[3] With the fall of the Soviet Union, the US interest in CD dominated over others and led to the stalling of the ad hoc committee's re-establishment since 1994. PAROS went into the backburner for the remaining part of the decade. However, the Bush administration's emergence into power in the US changed the existing situation, as they pursued an aggressive, neo-conservative policy on space militarisation and weaponisation.

In January 2001, a Congressionally mandated space commission headed by Donald Rumsfeld under the Bush administration recommended, The US government should vigorously pursue the capabilities called for in the National Space Policy to ensure that the President will have option to deploy weapons in space to deter threats to, and, if necessary, defend against attacks on US interests. As expected, the US withdrew from the ABM (Anti Ballistic Missile) treaty in 2002.[4] The Air Force Space Command in its 2003 Strategic Master Plan suggested that the 'ability to gain space superiority (the ability to exploit space while selectively disallowing it to adversaries) is critically important and maintaining space superiority is an essential prerequisite in modern warfare'. The 2006 US National Space Policy further declared that the US will 'preserve its rights, capabilities, and freedom of action in space; dissuade or deter others from either impeding those rights or developing capabilities intending to do so; take those actions necessary to protect its space capabilities; respond to interference; and deny, if necessary, adversaries the use of space capabilities hostile to US national interests'. The US also went further ahead in the document to express its strong opposition to PAROS by stating that 'proposed arms control agreements or restrictions must not impair the rights of the United States to conduct research, development, testing, and operations or other activities in space for US national interests'. In the same year, a US representative re-emphasised the nation's stand that 'there is no – repeat, no – problem in outer space for arms control to solve'.[5]

The first step by the US during this period on space weaponisation was through the deployment of ground-based mid-course Missile Defence System. According to the Chinese experts, the interceptors of this system, which is based in Alaska and California, could be capable of attacking Chinese satellites. The first experimental space-based interceptor test bed is expected to be deployed by 2012 by the Pentagon. In 2013, the Pentagon is expected to launch its first Near Field Infra Red Experiment (NFIRE) satellite to gather information on Ballistic Missiles, which also presents an opportunity for the introduction of a kill vehicle in its payload. The US had been researching on a Space Based Laser (SBL) for enhancing its Missile Defence System, but got cancelled in 2002. The US Air Force has also developed an Experimental Satellite System (XSS) to conduct proximity operations on other satellites, and was launched on April 2010. Such proximity operations also include the capability to attack along with the harmless activities of inspection and servicing. The US was also going ahead with its Shriever war games conducted by the Air Force in 2001, 2003 and 2005 in close co-operation with Japan. These moves by the US have hampered any attempts against space weaponisation, and is seen by China as threatening behaviour. [6] On February 20, 2008, the US itself tested an ASAT on its own spy satellite using a three stage Standard Missile-3 (SM-3) interceptor, which was used in the US Navy's missile defence system.[7] This happened one year after China tested its ASAT and hardly a month after China put forward the treaty for the Prevention of the Placement of Weapons in Outer Space (PPWT). By this move, the US appeared to signal to China that it is also capable of responding offensively or defensively against the Chinese space assets in case of any eventuality. The US wanted to demonstrate to China that its ASAT arsenal is well in place and its intent to use it on China. The US also wanted China to know that it will not give up on its BMD projects and will not support any multilateral initiatives to cap its developing capabilities in the sector.

The 2010 US National Space Policy under President Obama have been more accommodative of the negotiations, at least in rhetoric. It indirectly declared its readiness to pursue the negotiations on treaties like the PAROS only if the essential criteria of 'equitability, effective verifiability and enhancement of the national security interests of the US and its allies' are met. According to the US, the Sino-Russian joint draft treaty on the PPWT does not meet these three vital requirements.[8] Therefore, as per the US, it cannot be treated as a base from which further negotiations can take place.

China and the Paros Treaty Negotiations

China acceded to the Outer Space Treaty in December 1983, and since 1984 have been consistently introducing draft resolutions on the PAROS in UNGA. China has also been seeking a PAROS treaty to be negotiated at the CD. In its 1998 as well as 2000 White Paper on national defence, China had called for the creation of a multilateral regime for the PAROS. China has specifically mentioned in its White papers on National Defence consistently that it seeks the ban on experimentation, production and deployment of weapons of all kinds in space, including anti-missile and anti-satellite weapons as soon as possible through a legally binding international agreement. Despite the rhetoric, China itself had been working on such weapons.[9] In 2000, China submitted to the CD a working paper 'China's Position on and Suggestions for Ways to Address the Issue of Prevention of an Arms Race in Outer Space at the Conference on Disarmament'. It called upon CD to make PAROS as one of the top priorities in its agenda.[10]

Post the ABM withdrawal by the US, China has been shifting its stand on space security from that of militarisation of space to its weaponisation since 2002. Evidently, China has become wary of the US not abiding by the majority decision of the international community to ban space weaponisation. It desperately began seeking a two pronged strategy – pushing for the PAROS at one end and at the same time, taking into account its defence requirements on the other end. This has been consistent with its own advances in the space sector, where it has been launching lately reconnaissance, communications and navigational satellites for modernising its military. It has been argued that the recent Chinese literature in the domain has been becoming assertive over controlling space in way no different than controlling the Exclusive Economic Zones (EEZs) in the maritime domain. In addition to this extension of sovereign space, they also suggest that the war doctrines of the high seas are being transplanted into outer space.[11] China's working paper to the CD states, Only a treaty based prohibition of the deployment of weapons in outer space and the prevention of the threat or use of force against outer space objects can eliminate the emerging threat of an arms race in outer space and ensure the security for outer space assets of all countries, which is an essential condition for the maintenance of world peace. China is joined by Russia on this effort, having placed a moratorium on its space weapons programme in the 1980s. The US response to this call has been one of indifference.

China and Russia became concerned partners with a shared threat perception coming from the imminent US BMD plans. They decided to re-invigorate the PAROS debate at CD; in 2002, China and Russia jointly attempted to end the ongoing deadlock by submitting a joint working paper to the CD. This move gave a fresh impetus to the discussions on the PAROS. This paper put forward certain specific proposals on the major elements for the future international legal agreement. In 2004, China and Russia again jointly came up, this time with two thematic papers at the CD, called the 'Existing International Legal Instruments and the Prevention of the Weaponisation of Outer Space' and the 'Verification aspects of Prevention of an Arms Race in Outer Space'. Both the nations again joined forces for the August 2005 meeting, which were hosted by the duo in Geneva, on 'Safeguarding Outer Space Security: Prevention of an Arms Race in Outer Space', but which concluded in an open-ended manner. In June 2005, both the nations jointly came up with a thematic paper at the CD, on 'Definition Issues Regarding Legal Instruments on the Prevention of Weaponisation of Outer Space'.[12] China and Russia tabled yet another working paper (CD/1778) at the CD in 2006, which dealt with the verification aspects of the PAROS.[13] There was a considerable momentum being gathered since 2002 due to Chinese and Russian concerns from US attempts to weaponise space. Both the nations led the front opposing weaponisation and assumed joint leadership of the pro-PAROS movement, the legitimacy of which came under question in 2007.

China's ASAT Test and its Implications

Just as the anti-space weaponisation movement was gaining considerable momentum, came the Chinese ASAT test of January 11, 2007. The formal acknowledgment of the ASAT test happened only 12 days after the launch, on January 23 after a period of silence as well as denial from the Chinese side. According to Liu Jianchao, the Chinese Foreign Ministry spokesman, while formally notifying the conduct of ASAT test, stated that the test is 'not directed at any country and does not constitute a threat to any country'.[14] But even before this, the China Daily came up with a mention on the test on January 18, which was quickly retracted.[15] The US Secretary of Defence, Robert Gates said that the incident was 'troubling'. Other official US responses ranged from 'very worrisome' to 'threat', 'provocation' and 'wake-up call'.[16] These reactions suggested a worsening of the situation in terms of weaponisation of space, furthering the US case on weaponising space.

There have been many alternative views as to why China proceeded with an ASAT test among those who were not satisfied with the official Chinese explanation. One is that it was timed to be carried out just before the Taiwan elections as a demonstration of its intent to both Taiwan. According to Lai L Chung, in charge of Chinese studies at the Democratic People's Party in Taiwan, the test was 'a warning not just to Taiwan, but also to the US, to affect how the US would assist Taiwan'.[17] Another view is that with this test, the Chinese might be arm twisting the US for signing a deal against weaponsation of outer space. According to a Chinese analyst Xia Liping, historically, when the US alone has some weapon, it usually refuses to agree to prohibit that kind of weapon.[18] Therefore, the Chinese strategy seems to be building pressure through possession of such a weapon so that the US itself will initiate a treaty against space weaponisation, as observed through US foreign policy practice. China is also requiring a treaty because it is also having an increasing number of assets in space to protect. But this approach seems to have backfired at least for now, as could be judged from the US reactions to the test. Thus yet another view suggests this as a sign of an assertive and over-confident China flexing its muscle and demonstrating its intent for controlling space and breaking the US monopoly over it. One more view could be that China has concluded that the US is targeting China through its military space activities mentioned earlier. Since the US is not ready to accept any treaties against space weaponisation, China must have felt the need to signal its deterrent capability through this test. The real reason may even be a combination of the above, like provoking the US into signing a treaty, whereby, in case it refrains the Chinese would not be left without the weapons on its side.

As a result of the test, it is estimated that almost 125 satellites are at risk from the thousands of pieces of debris created by the test, which could impact and damage them, which could have fallout on global information and communication networks. It is therefore affecting the space interests of all nations having a direct and indirect stake in space programmes. An ASAT test of this type does not by itself constitute a breach of any existing international treaty, especially with the Outer Space Treaty signed by the US in 1967 and China in 1983.[19].China was evidently well aware of the damaging consequences to space safety due to conducting an ASAT. The final stage of its own launch vehicle, the Long March 4A carrying its Fengyun-1(02) weather satellite exploded in October 1990, creating almost 84 pieces of debris in space. The US also launched an ASAT in September 1985 to destroy its Solwind weather satellite. In addition, China has been part of the Inter Agency Space Debris Co-ordination Committee since 1995. Based all these experiences, there is hardly a chance of China underestimating the space safety related repercussions of its ASAT test. In addition to this, China is also liable for compensations for other nation's assets, which are damaged by its ASAT test under the Liability Convention of 1972. China has hardly violated any international law by its ASAT test. No space law has prohibited a state to destroy its own assets in space. The Outer Space Treaty of 1967, as per its Article XI, had sought nations to 'undertake international consultations before proceeding with any activity that could cause potentially harmful interference with the peaceful exploration and use of outer space'. China has not conducted any sort of international consultations on its ASAT test prior to its launch, following the convention set by earlier space powers.[20] China has therefore been exploiting the loopholes in the international space law in its favour.

Just as the international community thought that China was about to backtrack from the PAROS negotiation drive, the exact opposite happened. On the year of its ASAT test, China put forward another joint working paper with Russia, which contained definitions on space weaponisation aspects, such as Outer Space, Space Weapons, Space Objects and the Peaceful Use of Outer Space. But the major surprise came in 2008, with China jointly submitting with Russia the PPWT to the CD. This was welcomed by the Group of 21, and called for the negotiation on PAROS on this basis. In 2010, they were joined by countries from other groups like Australia, Belarus and Kazakhstan, who welcomed the draft submitted by China and Russia.[21]

China knows very well from the experience of the Soviet Union that involving in an arms race with the US would lead it into a whirlpool, which would suck out all its resources and lead the nation to a similar downfall. China would, therefore, need PAROS so as to halt the US moves to create a National Missile Defence (NMD). As a backup for the plan, China needs to ready itself for the inevitable – an 'arms race' in case it is unable to coerce the US into PAROS negotiations. At the same time, the race for space weaponisation should cease at certain level for the maintenance of its strategic higher ground in space. Therefore, this means that any additional players should be preventing from becoming space weapon powers. China's ASAT test needs to be viewed in this perspective. The current and imminent strategy for China would therefore be to strive towards PAROS on one hand and simultaneously build up its space weapons to attain strategic parity with the US. This means, evidently, a lack of focus on the PAROS front for China, as it would have to balance between the two ends. This is China's current strategy as well as its strategy for the near future. From this view point, China's ASAT test proves to be a rational and practical measure which should have been taken in the best national security and strategic interests of the nation. It also explains why China is pushing forward for PAROS at the same time, even after attaining ASAT capabilities.

Notes

1. The formal names of the treaties are the following: Outer Space Treaty - "Treaty on Principles Governing the Activities of States in the Exploration and Use of Outer Space, Including the Moon and Other Celestial Bodies", Liability Convention - "Convention on the International Liability for Damage Caused by Space Objects", Launch Registration Convention - "Convention on Registration of Objects Launched into Outer Space", Environmental Modification Convention - "Convention on the Prohibition of Military or Any Other Hostile Use of Environment Modification Techniques, and Moon Agreement - "Agreement Governing the Activities of States on the Moon and Other Celestial Bodies", see the UN Office for Outer Space Affairs (UNOOSA) website http://www.oosa.unvienna.org/oosa/en/SpaceLaw/index.html, accessed on March 25, 2012.
2. K. Lalitendra, *Militarisation of Space,* (New Delhi: KW Publications, 2010), pp. 30-40.
3. James Martin Center for Non-proliferation Studies, "Proposed Prevention of an Arms Race in Outer Space (PAROS) Treaty", *Inventory of International Non-proliferation Organisations & Regimes*, see http://cns.miis.edu/inventory/pdfs/paros.pdf, accessed on March 27, 2012.
4. H. Zhang, "Action/Reaction: US Space Weaponisation and China" *Arms Control Today*, December 2005", see http://www.armscontrol.org/act/2005_12/Dec-cvr, accessed on April 04, 2012.
5. Reaching Critical Will, "Prevention of an Arms Race in Outer Space: A Backgrounder on what is being done to Prevent an Arms Race in Outer Space at the UN", see http://www.reachingcriticalwill.org/resources/fact-sheets/critical-issues/5454-prevention-of-an-arms-race-in-outer-space, accessed on April 04, 2012.
6. n. 126.
7. Ibid.
8. Reaching Critical Will, "Preventing an Arms Race in Outer Space: A Backgrounder on the Militarisation and Weaponisation of Outer Space", see http://www.reachingcriticalwill.org/resources/fact-sheets/critical-issues/5448-outer-space, accessed on March 25, 2012.
9. A. Sahgal, "An Overview of Chinese Space Policies and Programmes" in A. Gupta, A. Malik and A. Lele (eds.), *Space Security: Need for Global Convergence* (New Delhi: Pentagon Press, 2012), p. 26.
10. "China's Endeavors for Arms Control, Disarmament and Non-Proliferation", September 01, 2005, see http://www.china.org.cn/english/2005/Aug/140343.htm, accessed on April 10, 2012.
11. n. 124.
12. n. 132.
13. n. 129.

14. "China Confirms Anti-Satellite Missile Test", *The Guardian*, January 23, 2007, see http://www.guardian.co.uk/science/2007/jan/23/spaceexploration.china?INTCMP=SRCH, accessed on April 12, 2012.
15. G. Friedman, "Space and Sea-Lane Control in Chinese Strategy", *Stratfor*, January 24, 2007, p. 27.
16. B. Gill and M. Kleiber, "China's Space Odyssey", *Foreign Affairs*, May/June 2007, vol. 86, no. 3, p. 6, see www.jstor.org/stable/20032344, accessed on April 14, 2012.
17. n. 137.
18. E. Hagt, "China's ASAT Test: Strategic Response", China Security, no. 5, Winter 2007, p. 27, see www.wsichina.org/cs5_3.pdf, accessed on April 14, 2012.
19. G. Anzera, "China's ASAT Test and its Impact on the United States", *Power and Interest News Report*, January 29, 2007.
20. n. 133, pp. 30-40.
21. n. 129.

6. Challenges for India and the Way Ahead

China will certainly keep emphasising on its research and development in the space sector and would in all probability achieve its objectives in due course. The pace at which the development in China has been taking place in the space domain will, at the same time, have lots of triggering effect on India's space programme. India has also been increasing its activities in space. Both the nations have developed their own indigenous launch, control and satellite capabilities and are branching out into newer areas of growth. Simultaneously, there appears to have certain diverging trends in their developmental trajectories in the space domain. As both the nations increase their global influence, their capabilities in space will come to play a major factor in the areas where they compete against each other for relative gains. China's manned mission, ASAT testing, its lunar mission and its advances in the creation of a space station have caught global attention. India's feats with regards to its growing space launch and satellite programmes along with its recent lunar missions have also increased India's profile as an emerging space power. The debate, which exists now, is whether India will try to attain parity with China with regards to its space sector. A comparative assessment of India's and China's space capabilities could be used to evaluate the challenges posed to India by China in the space sector. India's responses to the growing space capabilities of China can then be accordingly evaluated.

A Comparative Analysis of Space Capabilities of India and China

The following comparison focuses on the major technological parameters involved in the capability assessment of a space faring nation. By analysing the relative standing of both the nations (as on end 2011) on each aspect of their space related activities, an overall comparative assessment can be built up.

Space Infrastructure

In terms of launch capabilities, India has a comparative advantage over China in terms of geographical location of the space launch centres. India's Sri Harikota

(SHAR) launch site near Chennai is located closer to the equator than the Southernmost of China's launch facility, which is at Xichang. SHAR is located at the 13°43'N parallel,[1] almost half the distance from the equator to Xichang, which is located at the 28°12'N parallel. This is of considerable significance for India with comparatively less to launch efficiency and economy, as the thrust required for space launches is reduced with the proximity of the launch site to the equator. As a result, India has the potential to economically launch heavy payloads to GEO, also offering prospects for cheap international and commercial geostationary launches. However, China is set to improve on its existing launch efficiency and economy through the construction of its newest launch centre at Wenchang in its southernmost province of Hainan Island by 2013. This site, located at would still be farther from the equator than SHAR as it is located at the 19° N parallel. China will not be able to build any more launch centres further south due to its geographical as well as geopolitical limitations. Thus, geographically India has a permanent leverage over China.

Where telemetry and tracking centres are concerned, China has an upper hand, as it has facilities distributed geographically over ten domestic and three overseas locations. In addition to this, it also possesses six tacking ships of the Yuanwang class deployed all across the southern oceans and two Tianlian series of space based Tracking and Data Relay Satellites (TDRS). Meanwhile, India has only five domestic and four foreign based facilities for the purpose. Even in the case of launch vehicles, China has a significant level of superiority. It has in its existing fleet, eight different variants of the Chang Zheng (Long March/ CZ) rockets, compared to the two rocket types of India – the Polar Satellite Lauch Vehicle (PSLV) and the Geostationary Satellite Launch Vehicle (GSLV).[2] India's maximum GEO payload carrying capacity is 2.5 Tonnes (GSLV), very much behind China's capacity of 5.5 Tonnes (CZ-3B rocket). China also has a longer tradition of indigenous launches, which started in 1970, an entire decade before India's first indigenous launch in 1980. In all, China has therefore carried out fourfold more launches (147 as on 2011 year end) than India (35 as on 2011 year end). Hence, on average India carries out only a single launch per year, as compared to China which carries out three to four launches. Even when it comes to the overall launch success rate, China fares significantly over India. China's success rate is almost 95 per cent, much higher than India's 80 per cent. This lower success rate in India is on account of India's failures in its GSLV launches, which gets magnified with the very low launch rate. Therefore, when it comes to launches and its infrastructure, India is found to trail far behind China.

Fig. 6.1: Comparative Launch Trends of India and China

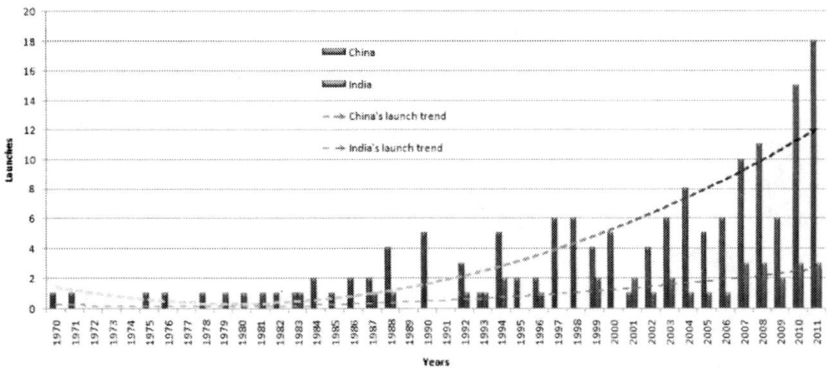

Source: ISRO and CGWIC websites

A comparative trend analysis of China's and India's space launches clearly shows the entirely different levels of trajectories taken by the two nations. Analysing the launch trend, it could be observed that there has been an initial lull in space launches of both the nations. Considerable momentum in the Indian and Chinese launches was gathered only after the mid 1980s. Since then, China's launch rate accelerated through the 21st century, and has been doubling every decade. In 2010, China carried out a record number of 15 space launches, matching that of the US for first time, and was followed in 2011 with 18 launches overtaking the US by one launch. However, in the case of India, the increase was at a highly sluggish rate. Compared to China's groundbreaking 2011 launch, India's maximum number of launches in any single year has never gone above three. China's capabilities in the launch sector not only eclipses India's but also cancels whatever leverage the latter has in its geographical position as mentioned earlier. This is because, China's superior experience in launches as well as its successful track record will obscure India's potential in the commercial satellite launch market. China would, hence, offer a more preferred destination for prospective customers especially in the developing world, who would definitely want to minimise the launch risk of their prized satellites, in addition to lowering the launch costs.

Satellite Capabilities

China gained a head start in the field of satellites, with its first satellite launch coinciding with its first rocket launch in 1970, unlike India which launched its first satellite in 1975 through Russia. Currently, India has 29 satellites active in space[3] which is much lesser than China's fleet of 82 satellites. India's communication satellites are one of its strongest assets, with a total of 195 transponders in orbit. China, on the other hand, has over 400 telecommunications transponders active in orbit. The maximum coverage among these communications satellites is larger for China, which has a semi-global coverage. India's coverage is limited to the Asian continent. Thus, in the field of communications satellites, China's capabilities are more than India's in terms of the number of transponders and the coverage areas.

However, in the area of remote sensing, India's capabilities are better placed. The information available in open literature points to India having more superior capabilities to China in this domain. However, since the space programme of China is highly militarised and significantly opaque, much of the information with regards to its remote sensing capabilities are hidden. The officially stated information points to Chinese remote sensing capability quantifiable to a maximum resolution of 2.36 m. Indian remote sensing satellites on the other hand, have a maximum resolution of less than 1 m, provided by the CARTOSAT-2 family of satellites.[4] It is widely speculated that China has, in all probability, acquired Synthetic Aperture Radar (SAR) capabilities. In this case, China's maximum image resolution capacity should be even lesser than 2.36 m. India has so far not acquired such capabilities, but is steadily working towards it. The RISAT-1 will be the first SAR imaging satellite launched by India.[5] In addition to this, India has only one dedicated meteorological satellite, the KALPANA-1. This satellite was launched in 2003, and is having a specified life of seven years.[6] Hence, this satellite could become inactive anytime, leaving India without a dedicated indigenous satellite for meteorological predictions and analysis. On the other hand, China has six Fengyun meteorological satellites active in both the SSO and GEO, providing global coverage. Four of these satellites are also included in the WMO's Global Observing System satellites. Considering all these aspects, in the domain of remote sensing it can be said that India is more or less at par with China.

In the field of satellite based navigation, China has put 4 geostationary and 6 non-geostationary satellites into orbit, to establish a purely indigenous regional satellite navigation system by 2012 and further extension into a global system by 2020 called the Beidou.[7] India does not have any capability in this sphere other than the GAGAN (GPS Aided Geo-Augmented Navigation) payload. This basically depends on the GPS of the US, and hence, is not a step in the direction of an indigenised space-based navigation system. India is currently working on the Indian Regional Navigational Satellite System (IRNSS), which will be initiated in 2012 and completed in 2014 to provide an indigenous regional navigational system based in space.[8] One major area where India has been largely inactive is in building scientific exploration for studying the space environment. China has a fleet of 13 scientific exploration satellites presently active in orbit for the above purpose.

In the field of small satellites, India has been more or less at par with China. India has launched amateur small experimental satellites in place of this. The current six satellites active in orbit work in diverse areas such as technology testing and demonstration in communications and remote sensing applications. The most important aspect with respect to these satellites is the fact that all of them have been made by the student community in India. China has also been developing amateur satellites, and has four of them active in orbit. This reflects an almost equal enthusiasm for space science among the sizeable amount of young population in both the fast developing nations, along with the governmental will to promote their involvement in the discipline. Both the nations seem to be aware of the fact that encouraging this fascination for space science and applications has a long standing effect on the future growth of both the nations. Both the nations have also been advancing in the field of small satellites. They have been able to develop pico-satellites, which are satellites, which weigh less than 1 kg.

India has managed to keep itself at par with China in the field of remote sensing and small satellites. In other fields, India has clearly trailed behind China in terms of development and growth of capabilities. China has marginal dominance over India in the field of telecommunications, and a complete dominance over space science and space based navigation capability. Hence, with regards to the satellite sector, a net assessment of capabilities point to a tilt in favour of China.

Human Spaceflight

In the domain of human spaceflight, China has an established the 'Shenzhou mission'. China's first test flight of the spacecraft was in 1999, followed by a series of test flights, resulting in the actual manned spaceflight in 2003. China also conducted human extra-vehicular activity in space in 2008. The next step in China's manned space programme is the initiation of the manned space station project, consisting of two phases – the establishment of a space lab by 2016 and a space station by 2020. The initial and most significant step in this direction has been the launch of the Tiangong space module and its successful docking test with a Shenzhou spacecraft in 2011. In comparison, India has not yet achieved the capability of sending humans to space. The first step in gaining human spaceflight capability is the development of a safe and reliable recovery vehicle. India has only been starting to perfect the general purpose re-entry technology through its Space Capsule Recovery Experiment (SRE-1) programme. China has worked on this technology for its recoverable remote sensing satellite, the Fanhui Shi Weixing series, almost four decades back.

India's effort in the domain of human spaceflight has so far been restricted only to the pre-project activities.[9] China, on the other hand started its work on the area in 1992 through the 'Project 921', under which the plan for the Shenzhou mission was developed and implemented. As China took over a decade to realise its human spaceflight aspirations under the military and single party dominated system, it could take a longer time for India under the civilian multi-party leadership and bureaucracy. Most importantly, it would depend upon the amount of priority that the Indian government gives for the human spaceflight programme. As far as a space station is concerned, it would have to wait for the successful implementation of human spaceflight. This is the realm in which India has hardly achieved anything even in getting any plans set up, while China has rushed forward in a matter of two decades. This clearly shows a lack of priority of India in this area, as human spaceflight is far less connected directly to the development of the nation as the satellite programme. Space programmes can function even without a human spaceflight component, banking only on satellites, especially for a development oriented nation like India. However, it acquires an entirely new dimension when it comes to national prestige and geopolitical status for a nation like China which aspires to take on the US in all fields.

Hence, in absolute terms of space capability, India is far behind China in manned spaceflight. However, considering national priorities and the system of governance, India's path appears to diverge at this point from that of China. Democratic nations find it difficult to give adequate priority to sending humans in space, because of public and political opposition due to its perceived extravagance. The only exception in this case among space powers is US. This was because, the US considered sending humans to space a top priority only on account of the Cold War era competition which it had with the Soviet Union. Such a situation does not persist in India between the two developing nations. Countries like France and Japan does not have human spaceflight plans due to the reasons which are not much different. In short, China is pursuing human spaceflight as it is a single party driven, increasingly techno-nationalist state which is all set to compete with US. India is not, as it has other priorities rooted in its national development. Where it has scope to compete with China is, therefore, not in sending humans to space, but putting satellites into space.

Space Exploration

In the field of space exploration, both India and China have sent spacecrafts to orbit the moon. Lunar exploration is significant not only because of the scientific interests attached to it, but also due to the economic opportunities arising from it. Apart from the conditions of vacuum and low gravity which could help in the production of substances with a high degree of purity not possible on earth, it also provides valuable minerals and energy resources. The Helium-3 isotope is by far the most prominent among them. This is because it could be used as a fuel for Nuclear Fusion, considered to be a promising panacea for energy security without pollution risks in the post-Fukushima era. The Moon could also be used as a future base for further deep space exploration activities due to the low gravity conditions facilitating easy launches. China did it in 2007 and 2010 through its Chang'e-1 and Chang'e-2, and India did it one year after through its Chandrayaan-1. China has articulated its plan in three stages – an orbiter, followed by a lander and a rover, and finally lunar sample collection and return. The second stage of the Chang'e programme which involves a robotic rover is expected to be launched in 2013. This rover would detect, collect and analyse lunar surface samples. The third stage for collection of lunar samples will be launched by 2017. India's joint rover-lander mission with Russia corresponds to this second stage of Chang'e mission, and will be launched during 2012-13.[10] China's proposed manned lunar landing will happen sometime around 2025.

China has also ventured to explore Mars through the Yinghuo-1 probe mission in 2011, which failed. The next such mission is apparently possible only by 2016.[11] India does not appear to be interested in exploring Mars, probably due to its lack of any direct connection with the nation's development. China has developed and launched two mini satellites jointly with Europe for the first time as part of the 'Double Star' project for the purpose of probing and predicting geomagnetic storms or solar winds which is one of the major factors causing disruptions in satellite operations. India is also planning a similar mission through the Aditya-1 probe by 2013-14.[12] This mission is significant for India and China in terms of safety of their space assets. Therefore, in the overall space exploration domain, it can be concluded that India has managed to reach some sort of parity with China.

International and Commercial Launches

A comparison of the international and commercial launches gives an idea about the relative status of both the nations in the overall space launch business. India started its international launches in 1999, more than a decade after China stepped in to utilise the space launch market in 1987. Through its 9 launches, India has placed in the orbit a total of 26 foreign satellites, almost 14 of them being nano-satellites, which weigh less than 10 kg.[13] On the other hand, China has launched 35 commercial satellites into space. India, through these launches has served 16 nations, compared to China which has served 14 nations and a few multinational consortiums. The main highlight of India's commercial launches is its 100 per cent success rate. There was not even a single failure in carrying a foreign satellite through India's indigenous rockets.[14] On the other hand, China's success rate is 90 per cent, with the failures almost stalling the growth of the entire space programme. This was especially the case with the IntelSat launch failure in 1996 which kicked off a chain of events which apparently compromised US technology transfer regimes leading to the US imposing sanctions on China's space programme.[15] As a result of this, the West almost stopped launching satellites through China. This has led to China aggressively courting the developing world nations like Pakistan, Venezuela, Nigeria, Bolivia and Laos among others for both developing as well as launching their satellites at low costs. China has thus turned a crisis to its advantage by becoming a leading service provider among space aspirant nations in the developed world.

India's foreign launch programme, which had a comparatively smoother relation with the Western world, continues to provide them service. However, there are currently only a few takers for India's launch services among the developing world as China is increasingly monopolising the domain. So, it can be inferred that India's commercial space programme operates at an entirely different market than China's, although equally effective. While India's customer base is mostly the developed world, China's customer base is increasingly from the developing world. The economically-rising developing world is undoubtedly a huge market for space services, but the developed world will also be looking towards minimising cost and outsourcing launches as they undergo economic crisis and decline.

Anti-Satellite Capabilities

China tested its ASAT on January 11, 2007 by bringing down one of its own defunct weather satellites through a kinetic kill device. This development was viewed worldwide through major concerns on space security, especially in the absence of any treaty banning weaponisation of space. There have been fears that other nations would follow suit, provoked by China's ASAT demonstration. China might have its own justification and rationale for conducting the test and endangering the safety of the space assets of other nations. However, the test stands as a stark reminder to the need for India to create a suitable deterrent so that its own assets would not be targeted by any country. Any such targeted attacks could put the nation's security under great risk. There is much ambiguity regarding the development of such weapons by India for its own defence.

On the issue of development of ASAT technologies, V.K. Saraswat, the chief of India's Defence Research and Development Organisation (DRDO), declared, India is putting together building blocks of technology that could be used to neutralize enemy satellites. He also added that India has started planning such technology which could be used to build a weapon in case the country needed it.[16] India's defence ministry's 'Technology Perspective and Capability Roadmap' released in 2010 also focuses on developing the ASAT weapons for the nation's security.[17] Therefore, in all probability, India might develop the weapon, but the only question which remains is that of testing. The decision to test ASAT like China is of very high physical and geopolitical risk, in fact more risky than a nuclear test. This is because unlike a nuclear test, the ASAT test has immediate as well as long lasting safety ramifications for the space assets of other nations.

Table-6.1: Comparison of India and China in Space Capabilities

Parameters	India	China
Launch Infrastructure		
Maximum equatorial proximity of launch centre	13°43′N (SHAR)	28°12'N (Xichang - existing) 19°37' N (Wenchang - by 2013)
Number of tracking centres	5 domestic and 4 foreign	10 domestic, 3 overseas, 6 marine and 2 space based
Existing LV types	2	8
First rocket Launch	in 1979	in 1970
Total launches	35	147
Average number of launches/year	1.06	3.5
Maximum number of launches/year	3	18
GTO payload capacity	2.5 Tonnes	5.5 Tonnes
Overall success rate	80%	95%
Satellite capabilities		
First satellite launch	1975	in 1970
Active satellites	29	82
Total number of transponders	195	more than 400
Maximum coverage of communication satellites	Continental	Semi-global
Highest resolution	< 1 m	2.36 m
Synthetic Aperture Radar capability	RISAT-1 (2012)	assumed
Meteorological satellites	1	5
Navigation system	IRNSS (by 2014)	Beidou (regional coverage by 2012 and global coverage by 2020)
Space science satellites	Not in orbit	13
Amateur satellites	6	4
Smallest satellite launched	Picosatellite (2010)	Picosatellite (2010)
Human spaceflight		
Re-entry capsule	in 2007	in 1975
Manned spacecraft	Not yet achieved	in 1999
Manned flight	Not yet achieved	in 2003
Space station	Not yet achieved	around 2020
Space exploration		

Lunar orbiting	in 2008	in 2007
Lunar landing	by 2012-13	around 2013
Manned lunar landing	Not yet achieved	around 2025
Mars mission	Not yet achieved	post 2016
Solar activity probe	Aditya-1 (by 2013-14)	Double star satellite programme (since 2003-04)
International and commercial launches		
First launch	in 1999	in 1987
Number of commercial launches	9	35
Number of commercial satellites launched	26	35
Launch Success rate	100	90
ASAT capability	Not yet achieved	in 2007

Options for India

The main challenge before India on the developments happening in China's space sector is whether it should go for a space race with China. There are different views to analyse this issue. From a domestic development perspective, there is no need for India to go into a space race with China, as India's space programme should cater to the domestic development of India. There are a lot of internal developmental problems in India which the space programme can solve, including the enhancement of connectivity, education, land use, environmental protection and prediction of natural disasters. From an economic perspective, there is a need for space race so as to capitalise on the increase in demand in the global space launch market. At the same time, India should seek parity and more so as to make Indian industry technologically and economically competitive. Since India and China are economic competitors and because of the significant political and strategic roadblocks in co-operation, it becomes almost a zero-sum game scenario for Indian space industry to compete with China. From a national defence perspective, there is a need for a space race with China, especially with regards to augmenting its relative military strength with respect to China through increased reconnaissance communications and weapons capabilities. From a strategic perspective too, India need to strike parity with China so as to advance further and attain relative gain over its comprehensive national power as well as boosting its global status as a great power.

Since the Indian space industry has been basically civilian focused since its inception,[18] its applications are also focused on civilian use. India undoubtedly needs to cater to its domestic development. However, China's space programme has grown to such an extent, especially after its ASAT test that India can now hardly ignore the use of space for military as well as the larger strategic purpose. The situation in which Indian space industry has developed has now evolved, and the latest trends are militarisation and commercialisation, fuelled by a increasingly assertive China, both in the field of economy and military. Space has come a long way from being a domain of scientific curiosity and developmental experimentation, to a source of military threat as well as a market of economic competition. Decades of activity by nation states in space has transformed it into a strategic realm to project global geopolitical power, much like the sea. However, military activities in space should be limited to creating a shield for the larger interest of the domestic development, which it was envisioned for decades back. Similarly, adequate precautions should be taken to ensure that the systems remain free from corrupt practices, which hampers not only the national space competence, but could also compromise our national security.

However, there are areas where competition is necessary, and areas where it is not – (1) India should build its competence with respect to China in domains like the satellite sector, space launches and military applications; (2) India should increase its launch rate without any sort of compromise on quality and success, at the same time keeping on reducing the costs. This is essential to attract launches from nations in both the developing as well as the developed world, especially in the context of the ongoing economic crisis. India should also focus on building satellites to the aspirant nations in the developing world without any such capability at a competitive cost compared to China; (3) India should also market its superior communications and remote sensing capabilities to such nations in Asia, Africa and Latin America, lacking in developmental infrastructure, by leasing transponders as well as providing imagery for their own national development, also at a competitive cost with respect to China; (4) The indigenous satellite navigation should be pursued by India comparable to the Beidou of China so as to reduce its reliance on foreign assistance. This will come to India's help especially in times of crisis, when the supplier nations might withdraw their assistance; (5) In areas like human spaceflight and deep space exploration, India should grow at its own pace, judged by the net benefit which might accrue from these missions, and (6) In the field of defensive uses of space, there are possibilities of non-weaponisation of space becoming yet another Nuclear Non-proliferation Treaty, dividing the world into space weapon haves and have-nots. It would create an exclusive club of members possessing the technologies and dictating terms to other actors, from the highest levels of control – the outer space.

It could be disastrous for the strategic autonomy of nations like India, if China and Russia can bring the US to form such an exclusive club and closing the gates of space weaponisation for other nations. India should, therefore, attempt at achieving such capabilities as soon as possible at a very high strategic priority if it has to maintain its autonomy in decision making at the global level.

Competing with China in all areas of space can strain India's growing economy and will turn out to be a grave burden during unfavourable phases in the future. Therefore, with respect to an Asian space race with China, India should focus on the three key sectors – satellites, launches and defence. This space race should ultimately serve India's overall development, and should be achieved as far as possible through indigenous development.

Notes

1. ISRO, "Launch Facility", see http://www.isro.org/GroundFacilities/launchfacility.aspx, accessed on March 18, 2012.
2. Details of India's Launch Vehicles sourced from ISRO website, see http://www.isro.org/Launchvehicles/launchvehicles.aspx, accessed on March 18, 2012.
3. Details of India's satellites sourced from ISRO website, see http://www.isro.org/satellites/satelliteshome.aspx, accessed on March 18, 2012.
4. ISRO, "Cartosat-2", see http://www.isro.org/satellites/cartosat-2b.aspx, accessed on March 24, 2012.
5. ISRO, "Future Programme", see http://www.isro.org/scripts/futureprogramme.aspx, accessed on March 24, 2012.
6. ISRO, "Kalpana-1", see http://www.isro.org/satellites/kalpana-1.aspx, accessed on March 26, 2012.
7. China Aerospace Science and Technology Corporation, "China's Homegrown Navigation Satellite Network Starts Providing Services", see http://www.spacechina.com/n16421/n17212/c190292/content.html, accessed on March 28, 2012.
8. n. 148.
9. Ibid.
10. n. 148.

11. "Failure of Mission hits Mars Research", *Xinhua News Agency*, January 20, 2012, see http://news.xinhuanet.com/english/sci/2012-01/20/c_131370239_2.htm, accessed on April 03, 2012.
12. n. 148.
13. Antrix Corporation Limited, "International Satellite Launches", see http://www.antrix.gov.in/is_launched.html, accessed on April 03, 2012.
14. Ibid.
15. G. Xiaobing, "Blockade on China or the United States? US Regulatory Policies on Space Technology Exports to China", see http://www.chinasecurity.us/index.php?option=com_content&view=article&id=249&Itemid=8, accessed on April 03, 2012.
16. "India Readying Weapon to Destroy Enemy Satellites: Saraswat", *The Indian Express*, January 03, 2010, see http://www.indianexpress.com/news/india-readying-weapon-to-destroy-enemy-satel/562776/, accessed on April 05, 2012.
17. "India to Gear up for 'Star Wars'", *The Times of India*, May 25, 2010, see http://articles.timesofindia.indiatimes.com/2010-05-25/india/28300195_1_ballistic-missile-defence-capabilities-satellite, accessed on April 05, 2012.
18. K. Kasturirangan, "India's Space Enterprise – A Case Study in Strategic Thinking and Planning" in Raghabendra Jha (ed.), *The First Ten K R Narayanan Orations: Essays by Eminent Persons on the Rapidly Transforming Indian Economy* (Canberra: Australian National University E-Press, 2006), p. 188, see http://epress.anu.edu.au/wp-content/uploads/2011/03/ch1017.pdf, accessed on March 08, 2012.

CAPS 'Non-Resident Fellowship' Programme on National Security

With a view to reach out to university students, younger defence officers, and professionals (media/academic) interested in research on strategic and defence issues, but not physically based in New Delhi, CAPS has launched a Non-Resident Fellowship Programme focused broadly on **National Security** issues.

This programme is in keeping with the four core objectives of the Centre:

- Conduct future-oriented, policy-related research on defence and strategic issues to contribute inputs for better understanding of key challenges, their implications, and India's possible responses
- Analyse past, present and future trends in areas of interest to prepare the country as an major power in the coming decades
- Promote a strategic outlook amongst the widest possible populace through publications and seminars
- Spread awareness to stimulate public debate on strategic and security concerns in order to strengthen the country's intellectual capital.

The duration of the fellowship would normally be 9 months and can start at any time of the year. The scholar will be expected to complete a monograph of approximately 30,000 words during the fellowship while working at home/present location. Applications for fellowship must include a CV and a project proposal (not exceeding 800 words) along with chapterisation. The final manuscript will be reviewed by an independent reviewer for its fitness for publication. If the mss is accepted for publication, the research Fellow will be entitled to an honorarium of Rs 30,000/- and a certificate from CAPS for queries and details write to the Centre (e-mail: capsnetdroff@gmail.com) or by letter to following address:

Centre for Air Power Studies
P-284, Arjan Path, Subroto Park, New Delhi 110010
Phone No.: 91 11 25699131, 25699132
Fax No. : 91 11 25682533
Email : capsnetdroff@gmail.com